A Teacher's Handbook of Death

of related interest

Talking With Children and Young People About Death and Dying
A Workbook
Second Edition
Mary Turner, illustrated by Bob Thomas
ISBN 978 1 84310 441 4

Finding a Way Through When Someone Close has Died
What it Feels Like and What You Can Do to Help Yourself
A Workbook by Young People for Young People
Pat Mood and Lesley Whitaker
ISBN 978 1 85302 920 2

Helping Children to Manage Loss
Positive Strategies for Renewal and Growth
Brenda Mallon
ISBN 978 1 85302 605 8

Interventions with Bereaved Children
Edited by Susan C. Smith and Sister Margaret Pennells
ISBN 978 1 85302 285 2

The Forgotten Mourners, Second Edition
Guidelines for Working With Bereaved Children
Second Edition
Susan C. Smith
ISBN 978 1 85302 758 1

Children, Bereavement and Trauma
Nurturing Resilience
Paul Barnard, Ian Morland and Julie Nagy
ISBN 978 1 85302 785 7

Good Grief 1, Second Edition
Exploring Feelings, Loss and Death with Under Elevens
Barbara Ward and Associates
ISBN 978 1 85302 324 8

Grief in Children
A Handbook for Adults
Second Edition
Atle Dyregrov
ISBN 978 1 84310 612 8

Bibliotherapy for Bereaved Children
Healing Reading
Eileen H. Jones
ISBN 978 1 84310 004 1

A Teacher's Handbook of Death

Maggie Jackson and Jim Colwell

Jessica Kingsley Publishers
London and Philadelphia

First published in the United Kingdom in 2002
by Jessica Kingsley Publishers
116 Pentonville Road
London N1 9JB, UK
and
400 Market Street, Suite 400
Philadelphia, PA 19106, USA

www.jkp.com

Library of Congress Cataloging in Publication Data
A CIP catalog record for this book is available from the Library of Congress

British Library Cataloguing in Publication Data
A CIP catalogue record for this book is available from the British Library

ISBN 1 84310 015 0

Contents

General guidance on suitability of material by age

This book is written for teachers and those who have an interest in talking to children openly and honestly about death. Each chapter is written for adults to give a broad overview of the type of information that may be useful when talking to children. Age guidelines about the information found in each chapter are shown below.

Chapter 1
- Adults

Chapter 2
- Age 8 upwards

Chapter 3
- Adults
- 'The trajectory of death': age 10 upwards
- 'Dying and cancer': age 8 upwards
- 'Dying and AIDS': age 8 upwards

Chapter 4
- General information: age 8 upwards
- 'The process of decay': age 11 upwards
- 'Post-mortem examinations': age 13 upwards
- 'Preservation of bodies': age 8 upwards

Chapter 5

- General information: age 8 upwards
- 'State-sanctioned deaths': age 10 upwards
- 'Suicide': all ages (with care)

Chapter 6

- Age 8 upwards

Chapter 7

- General information: age 8 upwards
- 'Social meaning and function of a funeral': age 11 upwards
- 'How the body is prepared': age 8 upwards (with care); age 11 upwards
- 'Cremation': age 8 upwards (with care); age 11 upwards

Chapter 8

- Age 8 upwards

Chapter 9

- Adults

Chapter 10

- Adults: see chapter for lesson details

Preface

The aim of this book is to give basic information about the facts of death and dying. It is by no means a medical textbook, but rather sets out to offer simple and clear information about the process of dying and how death can occur. We consider funeral rites and the meaning of those rituals in society in order to make them accessible to children and young people. Our overall intention is to try to place talk of death and dying into an everyday context for children so that when they are faced with bereavement and loss they will already have a frame of reference in which to contextualize their experience. If they have further questions to ask to try to make sense of what has happened, the authors' intention is that they will feel more able to ask those questions knowing that there are adults around them who are prepared to talk about death in an honest and open way.

Death is not meant to be a secret or something shameful, but often feels as if it is. Asking questions about death for a child can seem like swearing loudly in a public gathering: it is something one should not do. We aim to reduce the fear and anxiety around talking about death and to suggest ways in which this might happen. This is not done as a separate subject within the curriculum, but as an integral part of the whole. The message is that this is normal; this is ordinary; yes, it can be sad, but it is OK to know and to talk about it.

This book explores how children grieve and shows how their natural interest in death can be used to help them understand it. The 'General guidance' on p.6 offers an overview of the suitability of each chapter for different age groups. The References, Further Reading, Books for Children and Resources sections will help the reader access a wide range of information and additional teaching materials.

Chapter One

Talking to children about death

Why talk about death?

It would seem that in recent years the subject of death as a matter of legitimate interest has begun to emerge in a variety of academic studies. Yet it remains a subject that, in general, we are reluctant to address. It has been a taboo subject and remains so today, but there is plenty of research to suggest that certainly in the first part of the twentieth century there was a willingness to look at the subject of death more closely, and even to consider how children thought about death. We will consider here both why that should have been and how we can begin to talk about death with children.

The reasons why death is regarded as a taboo subject are considered in this chapter, together with why there has been a shift in the willingness of some to focus on death as a subject that should be explored and studied further.

In the USA there are university courses in death education (sometimes called thanatology) and there are three such courses in the UK (see Resources). There is a Natural Death Centre based in London which gives help and advice to those wishing to find a way of making sense of their life and their death. We are becoming familiar with the notion that experiencing a death may require counselling or therapeutic input of some sort, particularly if the death occurred in traumatic circumstances or was in some way unusual and not in the normal order of daily life. It has become more usual for us to see the need to discuss personal problems with a professional who can help us make sense of life events. So we may feel that we are at ease with the subject as adults, though often we are less comfortable with the subject when we need to address it with children.

This is a finding borne out by the small-scale research we conducted ourselves among teachers, asking whether they address the issue within their classroom situation when a death has occurred within the school community. Many teachers felt that children didn't need to know anything unless they asked about it, but the predominant feeling was that they ought to address the issue but were unsure how to start. There was an assumption that particular skills were involved in talking about death to children and the subject should only be tackled by 'experts'.

We are more at ease with the notion of loss than with death itself. Our focus is more likely to be on the loss endured by the survivors than on the actual death. The focus of counselling is bereavement and grief. Textbooks on grief and loss rarely talk about how or why death occurs. Indeed the actual fact of death may be less painful than the loss endured by loved ones who remains to cope with the event.

There may be many reasons why we are less than comfortable talking about death. First, contemplation of our own mortality can be difficult. Second, as Kubler-Ross (1970) highlights, death has become increasingly less part of the fabric of most people's lives and the concern of specialists in death, whether medics, counsellors or undertakers. It is no longer the case that laying out of a body would be done in the home by someone known to the family. In the past an elderly woman would perhaps perform this function for most people in the community and often engage other women members of the family in the task. David Clark (1999) writes interestingly on the funeral traditions in Staithes in the early part of this century, illustrating this point very well. The possession of a suit in which the body is to be buried is no longer the norm; nor is it usual for the body to remain in the home to be viewed before the ceremony. Even with beloved pets we are happier for them to be discreetly disposed of by the vet rather than have them die at home or to bring them back with us to bury.

So we do not have a view that death is an everyday occurrence which is part of the lives of us all, but rather that it is a medical event which must be handled by those specially qualified to deal with it. This may be because increased technological interventions in illness have been able to prolong our lives and cure us of what might in the past have been fatal illnesses. It may be that as we become increasingly aware of hygiene we feel that death is a dirty thing which will contaminate our lives if we come too close to it. It has also become a something to be feared, even though none of us will escape it.

Death in society

What do we need to know about death in order to be able to make sense of it? Perhaps we should begin by asking what death is and whether it is different from the process of dying. For the purposes of this book we shall state that death and dying are separate, although connected, but that death is a point in time which can be located and has certain identifiable characteristics. These characteristics are essentially factual and a basic knowledge of them, together with a language in which we can discuss death, may help us to cope with the more painful process of grieving.

Death is not just a medical event. It has sociological and philosophical meanings and it can certainly have meanings in terms of economics, whether on a personal or global level. So to ask the question 'what is death?' requires many different answers.

The intention within this book is to consider death from many aspects and not only to provide the reader with factual information about the technical aspects of death, but also to stimulate thought about the meaning of death within society at the beginning of the twenty-first century.

It is important to recognize that although death is a biological fact – and in terms of the biology of what happens when the body ceases to function we can become fairly clear about what happens – the actual event is made difficult to cope with because of the social meaning of the death. We live in communities. Our lives relate to other people and even if we live alone our lives will usually impact on others in a variety of ways. It is rare for people to die without a social context, but even in cases where this does happen their lives and deaths are given a context by those involved in disposal of the body. In the area of England in which I live there is a large port where stowaways and refugees are frequently found on ships. Sometimes the conditions of the journey have led to their death and it is the duty of the local authority to dispose of these bodies in an appropriate and dignified manner. There are actually quite a number of these burials and the cost to the local authority is higher than one might imagine. Periodically, religious groups and humanitarians collect funds to commemorate the burials of these unknown bodies and gather together concerned people at such ceremonies to give validity to a life otherwise unmourned.

Roger Grainger (1998) suggests that in the funeral of the neglected and unknown we see the true value of this rite of passage:

> On these occasions it is neither an individual nor a community that is bereaved, but humanity. When the unpopular, isolated, socially stigmatised person dies and is buried with due ceremony, then Donne's famous sermon is revealed as simple, existential fact rather than superb rhetoric: 'Any man's death diminishes me because I am involved in mankind'. (Grainger 1998, p.128)

Why would anyone want to do this? Perhaps it is because we consider that the dead body of a person is more than just a carcass to be disposed of: it has a meaning beyond the fact of its biological state. Hertz (1960) suggested that this was the case:

> The body of the deceased is not regarded like the carcass of some animal: specific care must be given to it and a correct burial; not merely for reasons of hygiene but out of moral obligation. (Hertz 1960, p.53)

Death as a taboo subject

Death came to be regarded as a taboo subject during the second half of the twentieth century. There may be many reasons for this, although it is hard to be sure exactly why it should be so. At the beginning of the twentieth century, as already suggested, there was a willingness to research the subject and an interest in enquiry about the effects of death upon various groups of people. Perhaps the lack of medical intervention in many deaths meant that it was important for the individual to be aware of the state of dying and how to deal with the dead body. The elaborate and prolonged mourning of Queen Victoria for her husband Albert certainly created a climate in which elaborate commemoration of the dead was permissible, if not essential. It may be that World War I, with its brutal carnage, caused people to consider death more usually. After World War II came the inception of the welfare state in Britain and consequent improvement in the health of most people. We also see the professionalization of health care, not only in terms of general health, but also childbirth and death. Health and illness become the remit of experts. In 1959 Feifel wrote: 'Death is one of the essential realities. Despite this, camouflage and unhealthy avoidance of its inexorableness permeate a good deal of our thinking and action in western culture' (p.115). Many others have also reiterated this notion that death has become the new taboo, the shameful subject about which we cannot speak in public, rather in the place of sex as the taboo for the Victorians.

It is a powerful and distressing experience to realize the full extent to which we consider death to be shameful and unmentionable. Many people who have been bereaved will know exactly how this feels, as will those who meet with recently bereaved friends and colleagues. One doesn't know what to say, one is embarrassed, hoping that no one will mention it and particularly that there will be no demonstration of emotion.

I remember two events that illustrate this for me following my father's death when I was 14 years old. My brother and I were to play in a concert for an international festival two days after his death. It was felt to be important that we played, particularly as our father had been an amateur musician and would have been proud of our contribution to the event. The awful and shameful part was that we had to walk into a room full of people who knew that we no longer had a father. They looked at us as we walked in and the noise in the room decreased as we entered. No one knew what to say, and nor did we, so we said nothing and played as if we had spent the weekend at home eating Easter eggs like everyone else.

The second occasion was later the same year when the school needed to check that the contact details in the registers were correct. I felt sick as I went to tell my form teacher that he should make sure my mother and not my father should be contacted in the event of an emergency. He said he knew. He did not say to me that he knew my father had died. Before that moment he had expressed no concern for me – nothing. Clearly, this was a significant event in my life, yet no one at school had seen fit to mention that it had happened. There is a sense of shame and a feeling that one might contaminate others or that they might be contaminated by those who have been too close to death and so it is best ignored. It is very powerful, very isolating, and sadly an all too common experience.

So what is it that stops us from acknowledging that someone has died? Death comes to us all. It is not an unusual life experience, yet we behave as if it is something to avoid and be fearful of.

> We have shown the unmistakable tendency to push death aside, to eliminate it from life. We have tried to keep a deadly silence about death – after all, one's own death is beyond imagining. (Freud 1917, p.306)

Where does this fear, this disgust, this horror of death come from? We see death portrayed all around us in our daily lives. In the year 2000 there was a head-on rail crash in India causing over 500 deaths. During the weeks close to that event there were numerous bulletins and discussions about the death of John F. Kennedy Jr, his wife and sister-in-law in an air crash. A father and his two children were found dead in the father's car in a Welsh village. These are fairly ordinary samples of the news of death we are likely to hear at any point in the year: disasters, famous people, ordinary tragedy. Death in the cinema or on television is hardly something we can avoid, indeed it makes good box office.

I recently played the theatrical role of Joy Davidman in *Shadowlands* (Nicholson 1989). The story concerns Joy's relationship with C.S. Lewis and her death from cancer – played out on stage together with Lewis's anguish at her loss. The audience was completely engrossed in the story, painful and moving though it was. Why? Because it wasn't their pain? Because it helped them to think about the unthinkable? Because it allowed them to consider death in a safe way, or reflect on their own experiences of bereavement? The answer for each individual may be different, but death does seem to hold a fascination which both repels and attracts us. We want to think about death and we do find it fascinating, which is why we are surrounded by it. But to face it too honestly is hard, so it is easier to put it at a distance as in news items, to fictionalize and make it horrific and gory, or to beatify and romanticize it.

We can readily accept that death should happen in hospitals in the least painful way possible. We are willing to allow funeral directors to take charge of the final ceremony and disposal of the body of someone we have loved dearly, although we have become less willing to allow such intervention at the beginning of life in childbirth.

Birth is a messy business, and not without dangers even now, but more and more frequently we choose to take control of this life event. Yet death is still something that most of us regard as unpleasant and not to be spoken about, particularly in front of children.

Death as an ordinary life event

Margaret Mead (1928) noted that the taboo nature of death in western cultures was not universal. Writing about Samoan society she stated:

> All children had seen birth and death and had seen many dead bodies…they had often witnessed the operation of cutting open any dead body to search out the causes of death. (Mead 1928, p.110)

It may be that in the western world we accept the death taboo, particularly in relation to children, in order to reduce their fear of death. We have been ready to consider that children should be aware of the mechanics of the creation of life. Perhaps we are now ready to accept that understanding how life ends is just as important.

It has been noted that death is often experienced as a crisis. In order to reduce this state of crisis and distress we feel that honest, clear, factual but simple information will help both adults and children to begin to look at death as a life event. One of the reasons for studying death and dying includes the fact that it can help us to understand our own feelings and help us to consider the meaning of loss and separation.

This book sets out to reduce fear, not to increase it. It seeks to find a suitable way of talking with children about events they will and do experience, no matter how much adults wish to shield them from the realities of life. We consider the natural curiosity of children and how this should and can be used to help them make sense of the world around them. By increasing their factual knowledge of death we can create a frame of reference in which to discuss the painful aspects of grief and loss.

Key points

- ◆ Why talk about death?
- ◆ Death in society
- ◆ Death as a taboo subject
- ◆ Death as an ordinary life event

Chapter Two

How we die

Death is central to everyone's life. You could say it is the whole point of life. Most people try to live their lives as fully as possible before they die. In some cases we spend a lot of money and energy in trying to avoid death. Despite the fact that death is inevitable, it tends nowadays to be one of the things we talk about least and about which we know very little.

In this chapter the intention is to explain how death occurs in simple terms so that we can begin to make sense of it. It can be assumed that this is a complicated matter better left to experts. Indeed there are many complex matters that cannot be discussed here. What is important is that a basic understanding of the process of life includes an understanding of how things die.

What is death?

So what is death? It can be described as both an event and a process. There is a point where death can be said to have occurred. It is much harder to say when the process started. It might be described as a little bit like clicking the Shut Down function on the computer. We know the machine will turn off, but not straight away. It will need to shut down other functions before the operation is complete. At the bedside of a dying person the point of death will often be when the person has stopped breathing and it is not possible to restart their heart, though other functions will still continue for a time. A medical doctor who has to declare when a person is dead will perform certain tests to establish whether there are still signs of life. Some of these will be known to us such as checking the pulse or listening to the heart. They might also involve shining a light into the eyes to see if they react or even testing for a gagging reaction. In a hospital, machines can be used to measure electrical activity in the brain, although in most circumstances this is not necessary.

Signs of life

Before we consider how we know that a body is absent of life, let us first briefly think about what are the signs of life. Here we consider life only in terms of humans and animals, rather than plants, as it will be easier to relate to the immediate experience of children and how we can use some simple experiments in the classroom.

Breathing

This is usually easy to see in most people and animals. The chest rises and falls, and breathing can sometimes even be heard. It might be possible to borrow a stethoscope to listen to the heart beating; some toy stethoscopes allow one to hear too. On cold days it is possible to see the condensation formed by warm breath as it hits the cold air outside the body, or we can use a mirror or a pane of glass to show that we are breathing.

Heartbeat

The heartbeat produces a pulse as it pumps blood around the body. This can be felt in certain parts of the body such as the wrist or neck. By carefully placing two fingers gently over the inside of the wrist the pulse can usually be detected. Children can count the number of pulses they feel in 30 seconds and then multiply this by two to work out their heart rate. They may even do this at different times to see that when we exercise the body has to work harder than when we are sitting down.

Movement

Animals and people move by themselves or because something has made them move. It is easy to see this in larger animals, but not always so easy in smaller animals. Some are very slow and move very little. Touching or poking an animal when it is asleep will often cause movement, as many a family pet may have demonstrated – not necessarily willingly. Shining a light into the eye to test for movement has already been mentioned, and it is clear that the body will often react to unwanted or intrusive acts. Testing reflex movements in the knee is a common experiment which children can try out for themselves, although it is not always easy to hit the right spot.

Absence of life

When death has occurred the signs of life will be absent. Dead bodies do not breathe, have no heartbeat and do not move. Even when breathing has stopped and a person has been declared dead, some parts of the body continue to live for a little longer as each takes a different amount of time to shut down. Molecular death occurs when all the tiny cells of the body have stopped working, but this cannot be tested without sophisticated machinery. Usually death is said to have occurred when the heart stops and cannot be restarted, but brain death is the point where it is not possible to restart life at all. After serious accidents some patients may be connected to life support machines to keep their hearts beating because their brains are still functioning.

Some of us might be curious about how a dead body looks different from a living body. We might wonder if it looks the same as a person or animal who is just asleep. Initially it may not seem very different, but soon the differences will become apparent. In some ways the body will look familiar and it will be hard to know that it is a dead body. In some cultures it is common to have the body of the deceased in an open coffin before the funeral so that people can say goodbye. Often people say that the body looks restful and peaceful. It is not frightening at all. But the body is in a different state. It can no longer move. The heart no longer beats. Breath does not come out of the body and the eyes cannot follow, blink or react to light.

When a dead body is displayed it may look odd because it is both familiar and strange due to the lack of movement. The eyes may have been shut and the facial muscles may have relaxed, making the face look more saggy. This may depend on the type of preparation done to the body before burial. The body may have a pallor to it. The colour of the skin may be slightly grey or paler than usual, although sometimes this is disguised by make-up.

How we die

So how do we die? We will consider this first in terms of the natural process of ageing and wearing out. All systems tend towards entropy or disorder, that is they wear out or go wrong in the end. When we are young the body tends to be vibrant. It is growing and can deal with damage easily. But as we get older, repair is harder. Decay is occurring in some cells and some which are renewing get things wrong and are not quite as effective as they used to be. There are lots of theories about ageing. In a strange way science doesn't have a really good answer about why we age, but we know that we do. It seems that there is probably a possible maximum life span for human beings and the oldest we can be is about 115 years old. This might be thought of in terms of cars that are designed to last for a certain length of time. Some cars will be kept by their owners for much longer than the manufacturer expected. Others will be damaged and stop working much sooner. Bodies are a bit like that too.

The authors assume that the life cycle will have been taught to some extent and so what follows will be a continuation of that process; in effect it will be about how 'shut down' occurs in a general sense. First, we consider how the heart can commonly stop working. In a colloquial sense we consider the heart to be the most important organ in the body, even though this might not be the case biologically, so for that reason we start there. Clearly all parts of the body are interconnected and damage to one part will impact on all other parts, but we separate the functions here for ease of understanding.

The heart

The heart is mostly made of muscle, called the myocardium. The heart is usually about the size of a grown man's fist in an adult and sits inside the chest cavity, slightly on the left of the body. We have already discussed how the pulse crested by the pumping of the heart can be felt in certain spots around the body. That is what the heart is – it is a pump. In a sense it is like the pump in a central heating system pushing water around a series of radiators to heat a house. In a similar way the heart pushes blood around the body to different organs to make them work. The heart is divided into different chambers. The upper chamber is called the atrium and has a one-way valve that lets blood flow into the lower chamber, called the ventricle. This is the part that does the pumping. So most of the muscle round the heart is around the lower chamber that has to do the harder work. The heart could be described as split into two parts doing two different things. The right side receives the used blood and sends it a short way up to the lungs to be freshly supplied with oxygen. It then returns to the left side where it is forced around the rest of the body by the strong pumping action.

Within the heart there is a special mechanism that regulates the beating of the heart and keeps the rhythm regular. This is called the sinoatrial (SA) node. The heart has to do a lot of work to send blood around the body, but it also has to keep itself going which it does through a series of twig-like arteries that supply blood to the myocardium. Sometimes these arteries that feed the heart itself go wrong in the case of a heart attack. Over the years these arteries begin to clog up with material called plaques. When they form into clots that block the arteries they are called thrombi (thrombus for just one). These plaques are a yellowish colour and are made up of fat deposits, cells and connective tissue. It is normal for them to collect inside the arteries over the years, but sometimes they cause problems. When the plaques start to get bigger and gather together they can also start to absorb calcium, which makes them hard. We may have heard people talk about 'hardening of the arteries' as something that happens to old people. As these 'lumps' or atheroma collect in the arteries, they make less room for the blood to pass through. The arteries stop being able to help feed the heart itself.

When the artery is unable to supply blood to the heart in the way it should, this is called an infarction and the heart is deprived of blood. If blood is not supplied for long enough, the muscle cells in the heart will be stunned and will not recover. This often causes some pain and this is a condition known as angina. If the area affected is small, the heart will not stop but will experience a disturbance to its normal rhythm and then continue. It will not work quite as well as before because it will have to try to heal – like any wound we might have on the outside of our bodies.

Sometimes the damage and the stopping of blood to the heart goes on for too long and the heart is so damaged that it cannot recover. Sometimes when the blood supply is disrupted the heart goes into a sort of spasm or slows down and starts to pump in an irregular way. If the beating is rapid or chaotic this is called tachycardia or fibrillation. Sometimes the heart slows down and stops and then it might be that medical people try to start it again by giving it shocks to get the rhythm going again. When the heart is so weakened it cannot pump blood around the rest of the body and the blood floods back into the heart causing it to swell. Because the other parts of the body do not get the blood and the oxygen they need they will begin to stop working too and slowly the body begins to shut down and stop. The heart will try to work harder to make things work and will try to pump the blood round the body but only makes itself weaker and so in sense once a serious heart attack has occurred the heart will try very hard to work but will only make things worse and end up being the cause of its own failure.

The brain

The brain takes a lot of energy to keep it functioning properly. It is like the main part in a machine that keeps all the other parts running smoothly. In the brain almost all of the energy comes from its ability to break down glucose into water and carbon dioxide. A great deal of oxygen is required for it to be able to do this. The brain cannot store glucose so it needs a constant supply which comes into the brain through arteries. This is the same with oxygen. So if the supply of blood to the brain is stopped even for a short time it takes only a few minutes before it suffocates and begins to have serious damage done to it.

The brain is extremely sensitive. Just as with the heart, the way in which the blood supply can be cut off is often due to the arteries getting clogged, making it difficult for blood to flow easily through them. Damage to the brain can be caused in the same way as the heart through clots of blood preventing the blood supply from reaching it. The brain is very sensitive and any disruption in the blood supply will cause damage. Sometimes the lack of blood supply to the brain will damage only small parts so that some functions are lost but the person continues to live. The bigger the area damaged, the greater the loss of function, which in some cases will mean that the person dies. Damage to the brain can also be caused by a blow to the head or by drugs and poisons. Because the brain is the controller of all the mechanisms in the body, death is often due to disruption to the proper functioning of other parts of the body because the brain cannot send out its messages properly.

The lungs

The lungs are a bit like a cleaning firm. They clean the blood supply and send it back out full of fresh, clean oxygen so that the other body parts can keep working. The act of breathing takes oxygen into the lungs so that it can do this cleaning. If the supply of oxygen is interfered with in any way, the lungs can no longer do their job properly.

The body cells need oxygen and various foodstuffs in order to function. Oxygen is drawn in when we breathe in, passes into the lungs and is distributed into the blood to be carried round the body to the various organs. As the blood circulates around the body, the oxygen is used up and replaced by carbon dioxide which returns back to the lungs and is taken out of the blood when we breathe out.

The lungs need a certain amount of room and pressure inside the body in order to work, which can be damaged or interfered with in a variety of ways. If a hole is made in the side of the body, the pressure will drop and the lungs will collapse. With some infections the elastic tissue of the lungs gets damaged and cannot expand properly, requiring more effort to get them to work. This can mean that breathing in and out can feel painful and tiring. If the lungs cannot take in sufficient oxygen to supply the other organs, they too will begin to suffer. If breathing out becomes difficult and carbon dioxide is not released properly, then the blood will not be clean enough to do its work. In old people we sometimes see that breathing becomes more difficult. It takes more effort to take in enough oxygen and as this continues to be a problem it means that other parts of the body also begin to work less well as they are not receiving the right amount of oxygen fully to function.

As we get older our bodies begin to function less well and it takes more effort to do everything. Slowly bits begin to wear out and cannot be repaired. Breathing can be interfered with due to obstructions to the oxygen supply. This is called anoxic anoxia or asphyxia and occurs because the air supply is cut off due to the air passages being blocked or swollen, where there is pressure on the chest or abdomen which prevents breathing or if the respiratory system is paralysed by an electric shock or some poison. The breathing and functioning of the lungs are sometimes prevented from working properly because the blood supply is contaminated. If someone is seriously injured and bleeding heavily or their arteries are obstructed or blocked, this would stop the supply of oxygen to the lungs through the bloodstream. Oxygen in the bloodstream would also be reduced if a person breathed in carbon monoxide, for example, thus preventing the lungs from working properly.

The body as a machine

If we think of the body as a machine like a car, for example, it is possible to imagine how all the parts need to be working and looked after in order to run well. Some parts of the car will suffer damage or wear out but the car will still work, although perhaps not as well as it used to. If too many bits wear out then the car will not work. If the battery goes flat there will be nothing to give 'energy' to the rest of the car. Clearly cars can be repaired and have their parts replaced many times before they are no longer viable. So too with people, parts can be replaced, but sometimes the damage is too great and replacing a damaged part is not an option.

Obviously all the above has been described in basic terms and is by no means a medical explanation, but the purpose is to try to understand in a fairly simple way that we die because parts fail, parts of the body get damaged and parts wear out. This is normal and will happen to all of us. It is not unusual or frightening, just part of life. It would seem important that a simple, if not simplistic, explanation of how and why death occurs is introduced as a normal part of teaching about the life cycle before there is any need to consider it in a more complex way. The aim is to introduce the fact that death occurs as an ordinary part of teaching and as a simple and unproblematic fact. This does not mean that experiencing the death of a loved one is unproblematic, but it is hoped that if children already have some sense of how a death might have happened due to ageing or some injury, then the questions they might ask can be addressed within the context of them having some awareness of the fact of death and some words within which a death can be contextualized.

Key points

 ◆ What is death?
 ◆ Signs of life
 ◆ Absence of life
 ◆ How we die
 ◆ The body as a machine

Chapter Three

Dying

What is dying?

Dying is perhaps the hardest thing to understand and make sense of so that it can be effectively explained to children. It is always difficult to accept that someone is dying. Death is final. It is an event. The moment between life and death is brief. Dying can go on over a very long period of time. It is hard for adults to come to terms with the idea of dying. Many people can accept being dead themselves, but few people look forward to dying. Many will say that they are more scared of dying than of death itself. At the actual moment of death there is usually no pain, or so we are led to believe, but the process of dying can often be painful and frightening. The advances of life-preserving medicine do seem to change dying into something of a battle between life and death. Doctors and relatives fight to prolong life and postpone the moment of death, sometimes against the instincts of the dying person who is ready to give in to the inevitable. We often hear that someone has died after 'a long battle' or 'a struggle bravely borne'.

Dying can bring every emotion into play: fear, anger, joy, resentment, despair, hope, love, tenderness, intimacy. In this charged emotional setting, ideas and concepts have to be clarified in order to help us make some sense of dying.

The problem is to present the facts of death and dying clearly and at the same time to recognize the powerful emotions which lie behind the facts. It is essential that emotional needs like avoiding pain or letting fear take over do not force a distortion of the facts. It is equally important not to overemphasize the clinical details at the expense of the emotional content. For many people death and dying can be a frightening event, and it can be upsetting and confusing when someone we know is dying.

There are some clear facts about dying. The major causes of death have a very predictable pattern in bringing about the end of life. This chapter will look at two of those causes – cancer and AIDS – and try to explain how these diseases can lead to death. There are also less clear facts about dying, especially about how long the process can take and why different people are vulnerable to diseases in different ways.

The trajectory of death

We can consider the process of dying as a sort of graph: the trajectory of dying. It is a way of representing the speed of dying, which varies between people and between diseases. In some cases, as for example in muscular dystrophy, the trajectory is like a slow descent down a very gentle slope. In many heart-related conditions the descent is almost like falling off a cliff. In cancer cases the downhill path may be up and down like a walk over rough terrain, with sudden sharp falls mixed with deceptively gentle slopes. This makes explanation of how we actually know that someone is dying so much harder: the fact is that we don't always know. Sometimes people are very ill, recover for a time and then get ill again. But it is important that we consider dying as a process and not an event that can be predicted in terms of time.

When a patient is given a terminal diagnosis and told that they are not going to get better, it may mean either that death will be soon or that it will occur some time in the future. A diagnosis that someone is HIV positive usually means that the person cannot expect ever to feel totally well again, but medication may hold up the progress of the disease for many years. The person is dying, but very slowly. If someone is only expected to live for a matter of months, then dying has a much more urgent meaning, and there is the implication that death cannot be postponed for very long.

Sometimes we talk about dying when someone is very near death, perhaps in a matter of hours. Close relatives are summoned in the expectation that this is their last chance to see that person alive, and to give them the opportunity to be present at the moment of death. The exact pinpointing of the time of the impending death is not an exact science but experienced hospital, hospice and nursing-home staff with lots of experience will probably have noticed changes in breathing patterns particularly and will be aware that these are significant.

Cancer and AIDS are two very different illnesses, although the final processes of both are roughly the same. In fact most routes to death seem to converge eventually into the same descending pathway: the heart stops pumping good quality blood to the brain; the brain stops sending messages to the heart to keep beating; and both are due to oxygen starvation in one form or another. Cancer is the result of things going wrong from within the body. AIDS is the result of the body being unable to resist invasion from outside its boundaries.

Dying and cancer

Our bodies are full of cells. Cells are the building blocks of the body and there are 10 trillion of them in the adult body. Each cell consists of mechanisms to keep it alive, reproduce and carry out its specific function. In some ways the mechanisms of the body are mirrored within the structure of the cell and each cell has a life cycle from being reproduced through to dying. Two key elements of a living cell are enzymes and DNA. The enzymes are responsible for providing the energy to keep the cell going through processing nutrients delivered through the blood supply. Normally the number and growth of the cells is a highly controlled mechanism. Things like deficiencies in the blood supply caused by poor diet result in poor cell formation and disruption to proper functioning. The DNA, which resembles a twisted thread, contains all the instructions for the cell's development and its relationships with other cells. The DNA contains the genetic blueprint, a pattern that determines whether someone is tall or short, light or dark; in fact it determines every aspect of the body's function and appearance.

So each cell sets about performing its allotted task as part of one of the body's organs. As each eventually wears out, it is replaced by a new, more robust one. Sometimes something can go wrong in the life cycle of one of the cells, which is what happens in cancers. Cancer is the result of a cell getting stuck at the reproduction stage and not progressing into a mature cell carrying out its proper job. A cancer cell continues reproducing and forms a tumour or lump. The cells keep on growing when they should have stopped and the tumour clings onto the organ from which the first cell started to go out of control.

The tumour does not perform any function in relation to the well-being of the body. In fact it sustains its own life by diverting and using nutrients that should have been used by the host organ. Tumours not only begin to starve regular cells of nutrition, but also obstruct the smooth running of bodily organs which can be squeezed out of place and prevented from functioning properly. A tumour in the lung, for example, can start to block up the airways and affect the breathing, preventing the blood from being oxygenated. A tumour in the brain can soon interfere with its electrical transmissions and affect the functions of the brain controlled nearest to the tumour.

A cell can become cancerous at any stage in the life cycle before it finally dies. Cells gradually lose their reproductive energy as they mature. These which become cancerous early in the life cycle reproduce vigorously; tumours grow at a rapid pace and are considered malignant and therefore very dangerous. Cells that become cancerous nearer to the maturity of the cell are unlikely to grow very much and usually stop reproducing; the resulting tumours are generally not harmful and described as benign.

Cancerous tumours kill in a variety of ways. As we have seen, organs can be starved of nutrients through tumour activity diverting the blood supply to its own needs at the expense of the host organ. Normal cell growth is inhibited and existing tissue begins to die off until the organ itself can no longer function. Tumours can obstruct normal function because of their position and size so that the damaged organ can no longer play its part and starts a process of irreversible breakdown.

The tumour tissue itself can begin to die off if the tumour becomes too big to sustain its own supply of blood. Tumours are capable of strangling themselves. The dead tissue can become necrotic, that is forming a sticky, brown, pus-like substance. This is highly vulnerable to infection and can erupt causing internal bleeding which can present a further threat to life.

Cancerous cells do not limit themselves to systematically destroying the host organ where they originated. Cells can break off from the original site and be carried in the blood-stream to the next organ down the system. Stomach cancer cells move into the liver or pancreas. Breast cancer cells travel to the lymph glands under the armpit and then on to the brain. This process is called metastasis, which means that the cells are spreading. Cells from the primary tumour transplant themselves to another part of the body but they do not become the cells of the secondary organ. Cells from a tumour in the stomach remain stomach cells, even when they have transplanted into the liver, for instance, and would remain different from cells that had become malignant as the result of a primary tumour in the liver.

Dying and AIDS

Acquired Immunodeficiency Syndrome (AIDS) is the result of a failed immune system. To understand AIDS it is necessary to have some knowledge about how this system works, which involves knowing what external agents threaten the health of the body. The body lives and moves in an atmosphere full of germs, many of which are seeking to inhabit it.

Germ is actually a generic term for bacteria and viruses. These are the main enemies of the body. Bacteria (a bacterium) are the smallest living organisms. They have very little function apart from eating and reproducing. They need living cells in other organisms to share the nourishment, and in doing so weaken the cell and often infect it with toxic material. The bacteria that invade the tissues of the throat give out an irritating toxic substance which causes inflammation of the cell walls – a sore throat. It is possible to kill bacteria quite easily with antibiotic drugs like penicillin, for example.

A virus is not a living organism in the real sense of the word and it is not possible to kill a virus in the same way as bacteria. It is smaller than a bacterium and consists of a particle of DNA, the genetic information contained in all cells, which is surrounded by a protective coating. A virus has only one function and that is to replicate itself, which is a more primitive form of reproduction, a bit like the ideas we hear about cloning. To achieve replication the virus needs the help of extra DNA and must therefore penetrate another living cell and attach itself to the host DNA. This interferes with the smooth running of the host cell and very quickly the replicated viruses burst out of the host cell and the cell dies.

A virus cannot be killed in the same way as a bacterium, but the immune system can eventually stop it from penetrating cell walls and replicating. It is difficult to differentiate between a bacterium and a virus and the harm they cause to the body. Both can kill if left unchecked and allowed to destroy cell tissue in such quantities that the whole organ is effectively destroyed. They both reproduce or replicate at a much faster rate than ordinary cells, so the immune system has little time to organize its defences. The main difference between them is that a bacterium destroys the cell by taking the vital nutrients, a bit like a burglar removing essential possessions from a house. The virus just uses the cell's equipment, leaving it defenceless. A virus is more like a squatter taking over a house or, to add another metaphor, a cuckoo borrowing the nest of another bird.

The immune system is the complex organization of bodily fluids, including the blood supply, that destroys and repels germs. Human Immunodeficiency Virus (HIV) attacks the immune system itself. It causes an array of infections and malfunctions of the body's organs and is called Acquired Immunodeficiency Syndrome (AIDS). HIV targets the T-lymphocytes which are largely responsible for creating white blood cells and are one of the most powerful elements within the immune system. When we are ill the number of white blood cells in our bodies increase to help fight off the illness. The DNA in HIV conceals itself within the DNA of the lymphocytes and adds to its own defence by coating itself with a carbohydrate cover. In effect it tries to fool the body by disguising itself as a bacterium, thus activating the body's anti-bacterial defences, which are not effective against a virus. So it tricks the body into reacting in the wrong way. The initial effect is a rapid decline in the number of white T-cells in the blood. The T-cell count has become the main indicator of the progress of the illness. Once the T-cells in the blood are depleted, then the body becomes more and more vulnerable to bacterial infection. Even relatively harmless diseases become more virulent and eventually fatal because of the extremely weakened nature of the body's defences.

Pneumonia, which is generally easy to treat in healthy people, turns into an extremely resistant strain and is usually ultimately responsible for the death of many people with AIDS. Death from AIDS may be similar to death from many other illnesses, for example, if pneumonia sets in then the lungs are unable to function because of too much tissue damage to the alveoli (the fibres that transfer oxygen into the blood and remove carbon dioxide). This depleted blood affects the function of all the other essential organs and the excess of carbon dioxide in the blood affects the brain and eventually the heart. Death then occurs very soon after.

Dying from AIDS is also very different from most other forms of illness. First, this is due to the fact that the deficient immune system lets in more opportunistic infections than any other disease. Second, HIV has the ability to mutate and change its identity to avoid detection by anti-viral treatments. The twin attack from a mutating virus and a series of infections means that dying from AIDS is not a single process of deterioration from a single disease. It is like dying from all directions as bacteria and viral infections seek out sites to destroy all over the body. The lungs seem to receive most attention from tuberculosis and pneumonia. The skin can fall victim to Kaposi's sarcoma, a form of cancer that is usually very rare because most healthy immune systems prevent its growth in its early stages. With AIDS it can develop with ease because the body is too weak to prevent it. The central nervous system is vulnerable to cytomegalic virus (CMV), which also attacks the retina and causes blindness. It is also vulnerable to toxoplasmosis, an organism which often affects cats and can also affect the sight and infect brain tissue, causing loss of intellectual function. The list of possible infections appears endless. The trajectory of dying with AIDS is no simple slope. It is a roller coaster and helter-skelter ridden together, as the person with AIDS fights each different infection, but slowly weakens with each round.

The experience of dying

Knowing the clinical facts about dying can be helpful in understanding the emotional experience people may be undergoing when they are actually dying. Dying is both a physical process and an emotional process. Knowing the facts of how someone is dying and how their body is declining can be helpful in making sense of the emotional state of that person.

One of the first people to consider this emotional process was Elisabeth Kubler-Ross who worked in hospitals with people who were dying, mostly of cancer. She noticed that people seem to go through certain stages within the process of dying from first being told that they are terminally ill to when they are in the last stages of illness and death is imminent. She describes these four stages – denial, anger, bargaining, acceptance – in *On Death and Dying* (1970). Many people who have worked with the dying have found her observations useful. Although the stages are by no means applicable to everyone, they are useful guidelines to understanding the emotional process of the dying person.

It is by no means clear that acceptance of the inevitable is the only way to die a 'good death' and we should be careful not to overemphasize this aspect of the dying process. Many people would concur with Dylan Thomas (1952) who wrote 'rage rage against the dying of the light', which is certainly not an acceptance of death.

In recent years there have been many interesting and helpful accounts of the process of dying written by people who experienced a terminal illness. These accounts are available for us to read for a first-hand account of a personal experience of dying and can perhaps give us an insight into what the dying person may be feeling at different stages of their illness.

Oscar Moore (1996), a journalist who worked for the *Guardian*, serialized the progress of his illness and his feelings at the different stages in a column called 'PWA' (Person with Aids). This offered a moving and real account of one person's experience, as do accounts by Ruth Picardie (1998) and Helen Rollason (1998). A description of how it feels to be dying will always be personal and can perhaps only offer insights into what some of the feelings might be. We can never know what it feels like for us to be dying until we go through it – perhaps even when we are near death we will not know – but the writings and the studies of those who have worked closely with the dying can be helpful in making sense of what might be happening.

Key points

- What is dying?
- The trajectory of death
- Dying and cancer
- Dying and AIDS
- The experience of dying

Chapter Four

After death

In this chapter we consider the decaying process that occurs to living matter which has died. The chapter does not enter into philosophical and spiritual discussions about whether or not there is life after death.

We know that death occurs when the body functions cease. This may be a slow process or happen quickly, but once the body has stopped functioning it will go through certain processes of decay. We are aware of these processes in plant life and have all seen mould growing on fruit or vegetables which have started to rot. Milk begins to curdle and form a crust when it is left too long in the fridge. Apples begin to go soft and develop a musty smell once they are past their best. We may even have noticed animals that have died on the road beginning to attract flies as they start to decay. These are all normal processes.

The process of decay

The first thing that happens to the body once it is dead is that the body temperature starts to drop. The time of the cooling of the body temperature can be used in estimating time of death. There are some variations in how long different bodies take for the temperature to drop. Usually it takes six to eight hours for the outside of the body to cool, but the inside will take longer. After about two days the body starts to putrefy or rot and the temperature again increases. This is due to the activities of putrefying bacteria and other decomposing organisms.

Many people will know the term 'rigor mortis'. This is a well-known phenomenon whereby the body stiffens. At the time of death all the muscles in the body relax, but after about three hours they start to stiffen. In a living body the function of the muscles is aerobic and anaerobic. In a dead body the function is only anaerobic: oxygen is no longer being distributed around the body by the blood and the muscles now only produce lactic acid. Oxygen is needed to convert it, but in a dead body this cannot happen. So the lactic acid level increases and a complex reaction occurs within the muscles that turns the lactic acid into a sort of gel, which is what makes the body go stiff. The process starts in the eyelids, works its way through the face and then down the rest of the body, usually taking about 12 hours for the whole body to go stiff; later this stiffness wears off. The whole of the body does not go stiff because decomposition begins in some parts and different areas react at different rates. After a time, depending on the person and the ambient temperature, the body loses its initial stiffness, usually after about 36 hours.

It is probably only necessary to know that the body stiffens after death and not to know the whole process of decomposition, but this may be of interest.

The body also changes colour after death, called 'livor mortis' or discoloration, due to the settling of the blood or hypostasis. Because the blood is no longer being pumped around the body, gravity causes it to settle and in the places where the blood has settled the body will turn dark blue or purple. Although this starts to happen straight away, it cannot usually be seen for a couple of hours. At first the skin looks bluish and blotchy, but after five or six hours the blotches join up so most of the body is bluish. If the skin is touched at this point it will still go white, but after about twelve hours it stays a blue colour even when it is pressed. Changes in the way the eyes look also occur. Almost immediately the cornea films over and the whites of the eyes go grey. After about two hours the cornea goes cloudy and within a couple of days it goes opaque.

By the third day the gases given off within the body as it decomposes make the eyes bulge and much later in the process they retract or go back into the head.

Decomposition

We know that plants decompose when they are dead, as does meat that has been left too long. The body of an animal left on the roadside will begin to attract flies. In films and wildlife programmes we see vultures hovering above the dead bodies of animals. Humans are not usually treated in this way and left in the open when they die, but nonetheless the human body attracts bacteria and flies which help to decompose the corpse. Forensic scientists can use information about the particular bacteria and insect life found on a corpse to find out how long it has been dead. Different species arrive at different times and the type of insects on a body may be due to the circumstances of the death. For example, if the corpse has been severely mutilated in an attack there might be evidence of an infestation of blowflies, or their eggs in certain sites on the body.

After death and initial decay the body begins to smell, which attracts certain insects. The first to arrive is a group known collectively as Diptera. There are over 100,000 species of these winged insects, including the blowfly (Calliphoridae) and flesh-fly (Sarcophagidae). These insects lay their eggs on the corpse, most often in orifices such as the eyes and the ears, but if the body is wounded they will lay eggs there too. The Sarcophagidae do not lay eggs but deposit larvae instead. After a while the eggs hatch and begin to feed on the dead tissue. The growth stage of the insect will tell the forensic scientist the likely time of death. Some insects such as beetles do not feed from the flesh of bodies but off the bone, so if they are present the scientist will know that the body has been dead for some time since the beetles will have had to wait for bone to become exposed.

Post-mortem examination

The cause of death of most people is usually known. They will not be discovered in strange circumstances where scientists need to assess the age of the corpse by the bacterial and insect activity found there. However, some people die in ordinary ways but the cause of death is not known because it was unexpected; the person had not been ill and was not in an accident. In such cases (and others referred to later) a post-mortem examination is required, sometimes called an autopsy. This is an operation carried out on dead bodies, not just of humans but also animals.

Here we will consider what happens in an autopsy on a human. During this procedure a medical doctor will do certain things. First, the body must be weighed and measured. If the body is clothed this will be checked, and if there is evidence of injury the size and shape of any wound will be noted. The eyes are looked at as they can give an indication of how death might have occurred. If the person died through carbon monoxide poisoning, for example, the eyes will be pink. Each body organ is carefully checked and samples of fluid will be removed from various parts. Blood is taken from the body and can be tested for alcohol, poison, glucose and blood type. Urine can be taken from the body by a small incision in the bladder and this will show metallic poisons and alcohol. Fluid is taken from the spine by a lumbar puncture right at the start of the procedure. Then the contents of the stomach will be carefully removed. If the person is thought to have been poisoned the whole stomach is sometimes removed for further analysis.

Liquid behind the eye, called vitreous humour, is extracted. This helps to assess the time of death. When the pathologist has made all the necessary checks, the organs are carefully weighed and then put back into the body, which is then sewn up. The tissue samples will be sent for testing.

Sometimes within school science courses the use of dissection as a way of finding out about animals is done as part of the teaching. Although this is not called a post-mortem examination, it has some similarities with the procedure and enables us to learn about how animals function by looking at their internal organs. Children might be able to understand this connection. The strict rules about the circumstances of post-mortem examinations are explained in a later chapter.

Preservation of bodies

Mummification

Perhaps we can also consider how the post-mortem processes connect with mummification, a procedure we might teach about in connection with history lessons. Although the purpose of mummification is preservation, not to ascertain how the person died, it has some similarities in that internal organs were removed and preserved because otherwise they would rot.

Many children will know about the rather gory part of mummification involving removal of the brain. This was not preserved, as the brain had no significance or importance to the ancient Egyptians. It was removed by a long bronze needle through the nose, which meant that the brain was usually taken out in one piece. Next, other organs were removed by making a long incision from the ribs down to the pelvis on the left-hand side. The stomach, liver, spleen, peritoneum, kidneys and lungs were taken out. The bladder was left in situ and the heart was never removed. The ancient Egyptians believed that the heart was important for eternal life as it would be weighed by the gods and used in judgement.

The body was always washed. It then needed to be dehydrated, which was done using a substance called natron. Natron contains sodium carbonate which dissolves fats. The dried out body would then be filled with palm straw or sawdust, both to absorb the body fluids and to pad out the body to make it look more lifelike. More stuffing or padding of the body then followed. First, the brain cavity would be padded with cloth which had been impregnated with resin or lichen. Other parts would be padded in the same way. Because natron would have made the body stiff, it was then rubbed with softening oils before being wrapped in a shroud and then bandages.

The actual process used on the body would vary depending on the status of the deceased. We can see how there might be connections with the way we treat the deceased nowadays. In Britain it is not common for bodies to be preserved, although the procedure is used in the USA. Different funeral rituals and particular religious beliefs will influence whether or not a body is embalmed.

Key points

- The process of decay
- Decomposition
- Post-mortem examination
- Preservation of bodies

Chapter Five

Accidental death, suicide and other non-natural deaths

Not all deaths occur due to the natural process of ageing or disease. Some deaths occur because of accidents such as car crashes, while others occur because the person takes their own life. Whatever the circumstances of the death, it can be difficult to explain why it happened and to make sense of it. Not all people who attempt suicide do kill themselves and not all people involved in car crashes will die. Some people are put to death in punishment for serious crimes. With some of these situations it is clear why a person dies; for example, if hanging is used as a method of killing, the cause of death can be easily explained, although perhaps not why this method was used. In other cases it is less clear why the injury caused death, but here we consider what information might be of use in addressing potential questions.

Accidental death

The deaths we call accidental are those which occur in an untimely manner and have no organic root. They are neither caused by diseases, nor due to the ageing process. They can occur at any time, in any place, to anyone. This is always true of death, as we know.

It might be possible to put accidental deaths into a number of different categories, as it would be impossible to list all the ways in which death due to accidental causes might occur, though to define these categories might not be so easy. We might also question whether some accidental deaths are in fact accidental, but might have been predicted and were not prevented due to negligence, poor risk assessment or lack of concern. These might include accidents in the home, road accidents, industrial accidents, sports-related accidents, weather-related accidents. Sometimes when people die after medical intervention the death can also be described as accidental.

These are the types of death that children hear about constantly in news reports: ten people were killed in a motorway pile-up, 3000 people are dead following an earthquake; a child has been killed when the brakes failed on the roller coaster at a theme park. It seems that the ordinary activities in which we engage from day to day can result in death, but usually they don't.

Let us consider how people die.

Life expectancy and death rates

Nowadays the life expectancy of most people in developed countries is around the age of 75. Infant mortality has decreased by 40 per cent since even the 1980s. Apart from illnesses that sometimes kill, most people die prematurely because of murder, accident, suicide or lethal lifestyles. In the USA two-thirds of deaths that occur in the 0 to 19 age range are the result of murder or accident. Murder is less common in Britain due to more stringent gun laws and so less likely to be seen as a cause of death in any age group. US figures published in April 2000 show that there has been a 21 per cent increase in non-driving related accidents in the home or public places (see for example *http://www.trinity.edu/~mkearl/death-2.html*). The suggestion is that this is related to an ageing population rather than a more foolhardy or careless attitude to living.

In Scotland (GRO 1999) over 36 per cent of deaths in boys under 15 were recorded as being accidental and 25 per cent of girls under 15 were said to die of accidental causes. If we look at the next age group, 15 to 34, 43 per cent of deaths were due to accidental causes, which includes suicide and drug overdoses as well as road traffic accidents. In raw figures 324 deaths were attributable to road traffic accidents in 1999 in Scotland. Of the 237 where the cause of death could not be determined as accidental, 24 per cent were caused by drowning.

Accidents

Often we have fears of dying in a particular way. Some people have a great fear of flying because they hear of planes crashing. Plane crashes tend to be very dramatic and impact greatly on public consciousness as often there are very few survivors, depending on the type of crash. In Britain some people may have developed anxieties about train travel due to an increase in derailments and particularly since the accident in Hatfield in 2000. The numbers killed in these incidents are relatively low compared to other forms of transport, but reactions and anxieties about certain situations do not necessarily take into account the probability of the event happening.

Sometimes we might wonder why one person died from particular injuries in an accident while another did not. Often there is only one answer to such a question, which has to be that we don't really know why. There are some factors that will make a difference to the outcome of injuries such as the extent of the damage, which organs of the body have been damaged, how soon help was available and how healthy the person was before the accident. We have probably all heard stories about someone falling from a great height and receiving surprisingly few injuries because the body was relaxed at the time of impact; yet in other circumstances one would have expected the injuries to be fatal. Perhaps this only serves to show that we can't always know what will kill us, but the rule of thumb must usually be that the more damage there is, the more likely it is that death will occur.

State-sanctioned death

In Britain there is no death penalty, which is also the case in most European countries. The number of countries where the death penalty has been abolished increases each year; in fact over half the countries in the world have abolished its use, with 30 having done so since 1990.

However, there are many countries in which state-sanctioned killing is still legal. Perhaps the most well known is the USA where in some states, though not all, capital punishment is the sentence given for some crimes. This is something we can hardly avoid as reports in newspapers, on television and even fictional portrayals of 'death row' are frequently heard and seen. Reactions to the appropriateness of this as a legitimate form of punishment will be socially and culturally determined and can be hard to explain in a setting where this no longer exists.

Children may hear reports of efforts to have a change of sentence for people who have been convicted of a crime in a country where the death penalty is still used. We might need to try to explain why efforts are made to alter the sentence for one person and not another.

Hanging

We will come across reports of hangings in some of the history work which children do. We may seek to give reasons why this was considered a humane form of killing in the nineteenth century. This can be done quite simply by explaining how hanging kills the person. It can seem very gruesome from a modern point of view, but in a historical context where there was a belief that the death sentence was appropriate in some cases, then it can be shown to be a considerable advance in humane killing techniques for the time.

The design of the gallows was carefully constructed to cause the criminal to die in the quickest, most efficient manner. Calculations about height and weight were important in the preparation of the gallows to ensure that the person died as humanely as possible. The effect of hanging was not that the person should die by asphyxiation, but by breaking the spinal cord in the neck, cutting off the blood supply to the brain and thus causing rapid death. Miscalculations in the length of rope used would cause severe problems. If the rope was too long either the person would die by strangulation, resulting in a slow and unpleasant death, whereas if it were too short the person would be decapitated. During the nineteenth century hangings were public spectacles, but meant to serve as warnings rather than entertainment. The use of bodies in anatomical research also required a rapidly killed body if it was to be of service to the medical profession.

Hanging is still employed as a method of killing in death sentences passed in some US states and a number of other countries. The table of calculations developed in the eighteenth century in Britain is still used today to calculate the 'drop'. The weight of the prisoner is divided by 1260 to work out the drop in feet. This gives the correct force of drop in foot pounds to break the neck, thus ensuring that death is almost instant, causes minimal bruising and the prisoner is neither strangled nor beheaded. Death is caused by dislocation of the third or fourth vertebrae with the knot of the noose placed behind the ear to ensure that the neck will snap on dropping. Blood is prevented from getting to the brain so the death is usually quick.

Beheading

Again in a historical context children will come across the use of the guillotine as a method of capital punishment popular in France during the eighteenth century. Children will possibly be aware of this through popular myth and historical drama or study of the French revolution. It can be described as an efficient way of killing, similar to hanging. Once decapitated, the person cannot live. The criminal has his head placed on a block under the guillotine, which is a blade placed in a frame to guide it to the exact place to cut. This can be compared to other historical forms of decapitation of which the children may be aware such as beheading in the medieval period and beyond. They may know that Anne Boleyn was beheaded or have come across other historical figures put to death in this way.

Decapitation removes the head, or at least severs the spinal cord and supply of blood to the brain. If carried out correctly, the person dies almost instantly. The guillotine replaced the axeman wielding an axe as a more accurate method of beheading.

Defenestration

One 'state-sanctioned' method of killing which children may not have heard about is 'defenestration'. This appears to have been used particularly in Czechoslovakia from the mid-fifteenth century and the word literally means throwing out of a window. Defenestration cannot be said to be efficient or scientific, as the injuries sustained from the fall could not be certain before the person was thrown out. The person died due to multiple causes, punctured lungs, or internal injuries causing internal bleeding. Perhaps its lack of accuracy prevented the spread of defenestration as a popular method of disposal.

Lethal injection

In the USA the most common form of capital punishments are by lethal injection, gassing or electrocution. In the film *Dead Man Walking* (1995) we see the prisoner 'die' from a lethal injection. We see the preparation of his body with the use of a muscle relaxant to help avoid excessive movement before other drugs are injected. We also see the attachment of straps to keep him on the gurney, both so that he cannot escape and so that the body does not leap about in spasm. Again, although a modern system of killing we can see how science has been used to cause the death to be as quick and tidy as possible. There are three stages to this process. First is the injection of sodium thiopental, which puts the body into a deep sleep. Next, procuronium bromide is injected to stop the breathing. This acts as a total muscle relaxant and is used to prevent the body from twitching or jumping about too much, allowing the person administering the drugs to be able to find the right place to put in the last needle. If the body were reacting too violently this would be more difficult and might slow down the whole procedure. Finally, potassium chloride is injected which stops the heart. A heart monitor and stethoscope are attached to the prisoner so that his breathing and heartbeat can be checked to ensure when death has occurred.

Electric chair

The use of the electric chair is something children will probably have heard about, if only through comedy sketches or cartoons. It is extremely unpleasant since the effects on the body are clearly visible as the internal organs are burned. The body is strapped into a chair and often leaps forward when the switch is thrown. The body changes colour, the flesh swells and may even catch fire. Witnesses often report the smell of burning flesh.

Gas chamber

This method of execution, which children will associate with a historical period, is still used as a form of state-sanctioned killing in some US states. The prisoner is put into a hermetically sealed steel chamber under which there is a pan. When the signal is given, a valve opens which allows hydrochloric acid into the pan. Then eight ounces of potassium cyanide crystals are dropped mechanically onto the acid, which produces hydrocyanic gas. This gas stops the ability of blood haemoglobin to perform and the body turns blue. Within a few seconds the prisoner is unconscious and death takes six to eighteen minutes. After death is pronounced the chamber has to be cleaned with carbon and neutralizing filters. The body is decontaminated by the use of a bleach solution and crews wearing gas masks must release the gas. The body would be highly dangerous to the undertaker if this cleansing operation were not performed.

Firing squad

Perhaps the most commonly seen method of execution in popular culture is that of the firing squad, which is still in use in the USA. A team of five executioners is used, one of whom will have a blank bullet so that none of the team will know who the real executioner was.

Explanation as to why this is considered acceptable in some societies may be difficult. Perhaps differences in religious beliefs sometimes provide an understanding, whereas in other cultures this may not be the explanation. Not knowing why attitudes are different is sometimes the only answer we can reasonably give and it is important sometimes to say that we cannot explain why certain things happen although we know that they do.

Suicide

Suicide is literally killing one's self. The manner in which it can be done is varied. The result is usually to leave the bereaved feeling distressed, guilty and full of questions to which there are usually only unsatisfactory answers. Suicide is not a new way of dying but has existed throughout time. In the early years of the first millennium AD many Christians committed suicide as a way of reaching heaven more quickly. The Bible tells us that Judas Iscariot hanged himself when he realized how he had betrayed Christ. News reports of suicides of the famous are not infrequent. Yet we still struggle with the acknowledgement that this form of death exists and find it harder to talk about than perhaps any other way of dying. The purpose here is not to talk about how one might die from attempting suicide, but to contextualize it and consider that this is a way of dying which children will hear about. We need to have considered it in order to prepare our answers, which will not be easy.

In the early part of the twentieth century Emile Durkheim (1952) wrote an innovative study about suicide in which he categorized it into four types, trying to make sense of what might be the underlying reasons for someone to take their own life:

1. *Egoistic suicide:* resulting from feeling isolated and from a sense of failure.

2. *Altruistic suicide:* from the sense that only by committing suicide can one meet the demands of society, e.g. hara-kiri in Japan.

3. *Anomic suicide:* as a result of feeling redundant, alienated and of no use.

4. *Fatalistic suicide:* where individuals have lost all sense of direction in life and have no control over their own destiny.

These categories may or may not be relevant to the reasons people commit suicide, but they do show us that there has for a long time been a struggle to make sense of why someone should want to take their own life.

It should be acknowledged that discussion of the fact of suicide is still difficult. Reporting of suicides in the media is a controversial issue, since over-glamorization of the death of a famous person by suicide is known to trigger subsequent suicides as a sort of fame by association. Stigma surrounds the family and loved ones of the person who commits suicide and there is still a reluctance to name it as the cause of death on death certificates.

We feel that death by suicide is a problem. Clearly it is distressing that some people should feel so troubled that they find the only solution is to take their own life, but the fact of suicide poses more difficulties than death by any other means. Perhaps it is because we find it even more difficult to find a meaning and sense in the death of someone who has committed suicide. We seek reason and perhaps blame and this causes severe discomfort because more often than not we find none.

Suicide also offers itself to a wide variety of interpretations by those who seek to use it for such ends. It can be portrayed as a heroic act in some circumstances – think of the portrayal of Bobby Sands. His hunger strike ended in his death, but there was great anxiety (on the part of the British government) that it should not be used as a form of martyrdom. The suicides of the elderly are a cause of concern since there is an increase in the rate of suicide among those over 60. Are we concerned that someone has lost hope in life or that it shows up the economic problems of living longer which some of the elderly population do not wish to contemplate, using suicide as a way of controlling their own lives to avoid being a burden? Often a suicide will be described as a tragic accident. The fact that the person really meant to kill himself or herself is unbearable so we reinterpret their intention and assume that they accidentally overdosed on pills and alcohol.

As we try to make sense of why people commit suicide we can look at the various explanations, but these give us no clearer understanding. It is true that there is a tendency in some families towards suicide. Does this mean that a suicidal tendency or predisposition is inherited or genetic? Margaux Hemingway committed suicide in 1996 due to a sedative overdose, apparently brought on by memories of her grandfather who committed suicide. His brother, sister and father also died in this manner. Does this show us that suicide is a genetic tendency or is it an acceptable method of dying in some families rather than others? Perhaps some personalities are more predisposed to suicide.

However, studies have shown that the personality of the 'suicide prone' person changes over time. The proportion of suicidally prone personalities appears to be socio-culturally determined and not fixed. We notice that the suicide rate in the USA dropped dramatically during World War II. The suicide rate in Norway is about one-third of that in Sweden and Denmark, although the countries are ethnically, culturally and geographically similar. So why the difference? Perhaps all we can say finally is that suicide is a complex phenomenon involving the interaction of genetic, biochemical, psychological, societal and cultural factors.

Suicide is perhaps the most distressing form of death to discuss with children since we cannot easily explain it. As with all talk of death with children it is important to be honest. If a child asks about suicide we should tell them in as simple a way as possible that this is how someone died. There is no need to go into excessive detail. If we try to protect children from the fact that someone committed suicide, the likelihood is that they will learn the truth from someone else whether we like it or not. Then the fact will remain that as trusted adults we lied to them, whatever our intentions of protecting them might have been at the time. A very short answer may be sufficient for some children, while others will return with more and more questions. If we say that a person committed suicide, the child may ask, 'What is suicide?' Here we can explain that people die in many ways: from being very old; from some illnesses; in car crashes; and that suicide means that the person did it to himself. The child will probably want to know why a person should want to kill himself. Here is perhaps the most difficult part because the truth is that we never know exactly why. Perhaps an explanation might be that the person had an illness in the mind, but we must also ensure that the child understands that, as with other illnesses and other circumstances, not everyone who suffers from depressive types of illness will kill themselves. As suicide is complex and difficult to make sense of, we would not normally expect it to be part of death education as a matter of course for all children, but it should not be avoided when asked about.

Key points

- Accidental death
- Life expectancy and death rates
- Accidents
- State-sanctioned death
- Suicide

Chapter Six

Social aspects of death

Who might be involved in dealing with death

In this chapter we consider those who care for the dying in a professional capacity and in what ways this work might be discussed with children as a preparation for the actual death of a person.

There is a variety of people whose different jobs are to care for the dying and the dead and we may come across only some of them when we are bereaved. A person might be in hospital and involved with nurses and doctors who do not specialize in the care of the dying. Others may use the services of hospices and their staff or nurses whose specific job is to care for the terminally ill. Most people, whatever the circumstances around the death, will come into contact with a funeral director who may make all the arrangements for a funeral or simply help the bereaved to access the type of arrangements they want carried out. In some cases a coroner may be involved, or a pathologist when cause of death needs to be established. Among the many people who care for the bereaved are priests, GPs, counsellors and lawyers. It seems as if there is a whole industry set up around death. Yet it is unlikely that we would be aware of this before we need any of them; nor is it likely that we would have been made aware of their existence when considering a career path. This is in keeping with our tendency to keep death out of our minds, or at least at the back of our minds until confronted with it face to face. Here we shall consider some of those areas with which we are perhaps less familiar.

Hospices

Most of us will be familiar with the notion of a hospice and its work in the care of those who are terminally ill. Those cared for by hospice staff will often be dying from cancer, but hospices also deal with people who suffer from other illnesses. We should consider what care they offer and how this is presented. We may be aware of local hospices through charity collections or lotteries which they run, but few of us will have been to look round the hospice or be involved with its work.

In recent years hospices have moved away from the need for people to be cared for within a building called a hospice and have extended the type of care they offer to those who are ill at home and wish to remain there to die if possible. So hospices now offer day-care facilities, with a range of special services such as assisted bathing, physiotherapy, aromatherapy, massage and social activities. These facilities are not only for the care of the patients, but also intended to help the carers and give them some respite and support in the care of their loved ones. The aim of the hospice is to offer palliative care which encompasses the needs of the dying patient up to, during and immediately after death. It is an holistic care that looks to physical, social and spiritual needs. Most of us will be aware of the use of palliative care in the relief of pain and nowadays it is usually assumed that there is no need for anyone to suffer pain in dying where the right care is given. Palliative care is now an area of medicine in its own right and much research is conducted in this field.

The coroner

Currently a coroner must be a medical doctor or a lawyer with at least five years' professional experience. Some coroners are both lawyers and medics. The majority of coroners in Britain are legally qualified rather than medically qualified. The coroner is called upon to investigate deaths where there is uncertainty about the cause. Often the reason for a coroner's inquest will not be anything to do with the death being particularly suspicious, but because it was sudden and there was no doctor in attendance or if it was the result of an accident. The law lays down a list of categories which must be referred to the coroner.

When a case is reported to the coroner there are four possible actions that may be taken. The first is to advise the doctor that an ordinary medical certificate of the cause of death can be made out and the death registered in the usual way. The second would be that the coroner decides to discuss the case a little further with the medical people involved, but then decides that no post-mortem examination is required and that certificates saying so can be issued. Third, the coroner might decide that a post-mortem or autopsy is required and a full examination of the body will be made. The coroner then receives a detailed report of the results of this examination and if she is satisfied with this certificates will then be issued. Fourth, if the coroner feels that there is still uncertainty about the cause of death an inquest will be opened. The purpose of the inquest is to ask four questions and only those four questions: who, where, when and how? The inquest does not seek to establish responsibility for the death, nor to apportion blame. Usually an inquest will be held when the post-mortem has failed to reveal the cause of death or there remains some uncertainty about the cause of death. All deaths due to unlawful killing must have an inquest, as do deaths due to drug overdose, suspected suicide, therapeutic misadventure, alleged negligence and death due to neglect. The inquest has a jury of 7 to 11 people who are chosen randomly from the electoral register of the district in which the death took place.

The funeral director

Funeral directors, or undertakers as we commonly call them, are usually involved in funerals in Britain. Although there is no requirement to use a funeral director, many people feel it helpful to employ the services of someone who is used to making arrangements for funerals. The funeral director will usually obtain all the appropriate certificates required for disposal of the body and help the bereaved make choices about the type of ceremony they wish to have. Although many funeral directors appear to be family firms, this tends not to be the case nowadays as most have been bought up by the big chains. The name of the former business is retained in order to allow people to feel there is a more personal touch, a local name giving a sense of care.

The funeral director will usually have a chapel of rest to which the body may be taken and kept until the time of the funeral as many people prefer not to keep the body at home. They will also arrange the laying out and embalming of the body if this is to be done, assist in choice of the coffin and the number of cars needed for the ceremony. They will also liaise with the church minister or crematorium staff in order to book the service.

Not everyone likes to hand over these responsibilities to a stranger, preferring to make the arrangements themselves. There are no rules to prevent this and since the expense of a funeral can be very high this is often a sensible thing to do.

The priest

We would usually expect that some sort of religious ceremony would be conducted at the end of a person's life, but this is not always the case. Nowadays more and more people feel that, having lived a secular life, they would not wish to involve the 'church' in their death. It is part of the work of a priest to be involved in funeral ceremonies and in the comfort of the dying and the bereaved if they wish to use this service.

The priest will not only conduct the ceremony according to the particular religion followed, but will also visit the bereaved family to offer comfort and hope for the future. In Chapter 7 we look at the variety of rituals and beliefs associated with death and the after life.

Bereavement counsellors

Bereavement can often be a difficult and lonely state and some people do not have anyone to talk to who will help them cope with life without their loved one. Perhaps in the past the family gave support, or in a more religious climate this was the duty of a priest. Many people still seek help with making sense of their loss by using the services of bereavement counsellors. The most well-known organization in Britain is Cruse, which is a charitable organization dedicated to helping the bereaved. Cruse offers specific counselling for those who have been bereaved, rather than general counselling. Others may get help from their

GP's surgery or via different counselling services in their local area. Children are often missed out by these services as there is an assumption that they are not suffering due to their different ways of showing grief. We have seen how this can be a problem in other chapters.

A number of people may be involved with the death of a person, although this is not always the case. However, let us now consider all the possible people who might be involved.

Table 6.1 Those involved in a person's death		
Doctors	Nurses	Ambulance staff
Police	Coroner	Funeral director
Mortuary attendants	Priest	Carpenter/joiner
Stonemason	Grave digger	Crematorium staff
Florist	Lawyer	Registrar of births, deaths and marriages
Probate office	Socal security office	Greeting card industry
Caterers	Hire car company	Newspaper

Key points

- Who might be involved in dealing with death
- Hospices
- The coroner
- The funeral director
- The priest
- Bereavement counsellors

Chapter Seven

Funerals and disposal rituals

In this chapter we consider the role of the funeral in death and how this can be explained and made sense of to children. We shall examine how children often develop such rituals for themselves in play and the meaning of these actions.

A brief outline of the legal requirements which operate will be given before considering the meaning and the purpose of the funeral ceremony in the process of mourning.

When anyone dies it is normal that we mark his or her departure by ritual of some sort. In Britain this is often a religious ceremony involving burial or cremation with a service of some sort. Frequently children are not expected to attend or are actively prevented from attending, although this trend has changed somewhat in recent years. One of the functions of the funeral ceremony is to say goodbye to the departed. The fact that we mark their departure with a ceremony shows that even when a person is dead they still have rights to dignity and respect. Another purpose of the funeral is to mark a rite of passage, not only for the deceased but also for the bereaved. The occasion allows a show of public support for the bereaved and a release from their usual activities, if only for a brief time. (We shall see this more clearly illustrated in Chapter 8.)

In order to make some sense of the funeral rites it is important to consider the legal requirements and meaning of the disposal process and also to think about why and how we often extend this ceremony to family pets.

Legal aspects of a funeral

Despite all the distress associated with a death, when a person dies an official, form-ridden procedure is immediately put into action. Where the death has been expected or occurs in hospital, some of this process will perhaps be taken from the bereaved, but nonetheless the legal nature of registration cannot be avoided at this distressing time.

When death is expected and the deceased has been seen by a medic within the last 14 days, the doctor will provide a medical certificate showing the cause of death, which is placed in a sealed envelope for the registrar. The doctor will also provide a formal notice stating that the medical certificate has been signed which tells how to register the death. These documents must be taken to the registrar within five days of the death, along with a host of other certificates. The registrar will then issue a certificate of registration of death and a certificate of burial or cremation (two different forms).

Sometimes there will need to be a post-mortem to establish the cause of death where this has been unexpected, but all cases of unexpected death are reported to the coroner who will conduct an examination of the body to establish the cause. The coroner also issues a form that allows registration of the death. This would not normally delay funeral arrangements.

Most people in Britain still tend to use the help of a funeral director to organize the ceremony for the deceased and to help with the arrangements for disposal of the body. When this is to be a burial there are almost no restrictions about where the body can be buried, although most people still opt to use either the church graveyard or municipal cemetery. Cremation cannot take place unless the cause of death has been established, which again requires more forms.

Even though this process appears overly bureaucratic and an unpleasant and distressing burden to the bereaved, the need to carry out these tasks can be a helpful part of getting through the first week of bereavement. They serve as a function and purpose in a world that may feel as if it no longer has function or purpose. Usually the bereaved will be in a state of numbness and the world will make little sense, so this 'framework' within which one is compelled to function can serve to give an order to the immediate impact of a death, albeit distressing and paper-ridden. The registration and certification process clearly has a function other than merely helping the bereaved, but it can serve to carry the bereaved from the occurrence of death to the funeral ceremony where the formal leave taking is done. It might be considered as a secular way of marking the passage from one state to another.

Social meaning and function of a funeral

The funeral ceremony is at one level a rite of passage. We mark the departure of a life from this world, whatever we may believe about life beyond. The ceremony is to show our support, to share in the grief of the bereaved and to acknowledge the life of the deceased. We may attend the ceremony as a mark of respect for the dead or simply to support the grieving person, but nonetheless marking the departure is a need we seem to have to fulfil. Even when people die in circumstances where no relatives or close contacts can be found, we still hold a ceremony of some sort to mark the passing of a life; to acknowledge that a human being has been lost from the world, which of itself makes a difference.

Let us consider why children, often unprompted, feel the need to mark the death of a pet with some sort of ritual. This need not only includes larger domestic animals with whom we can make sense of a close relationship, but also pets such as goldfish with whom it may be more difficult to make sense of anything that could be called a relationship. Children will quite naturally and spontaneously conduct small-scale ceremonies for the death of a pet or even for the death of a small bird found in the garden. They may show curiosity about the fact that the creature is no longer living, poking it to see if it will move. They may show respect by talking in hushed tones on discovery of a dead bird in the garden and show tenderness in lifting its body, putting it in a box or wrapping it in some way. They will then dig a small plot and put the creature in the ground, perhaps saying a prayer over it, marking the spot with pebbles and flowers. They may return to the spot to dig up the creature to see what has happened to it – this will vary depending on the age of the child. But nonetheless they will have shown the need to mark the departure in some way, demonstrating an understanding that life is in some way sacred, even after death.

It may be that the children are imitating what they have seen adults do, although those who have never attended a funeral also do this. Children spontaneously acknowledge the passing of life in their play, even before they understand the concept of death as irreversible. Do they have a need to show the connection of all living creatures to some greater sense of life? Do they have a sense that lives should not simply be lost without acknowledgement of their existence? Certainly when they conduct such pet funerals they are honouring the deceased and giving dignity to their death.

Most adults are not uncomfortable with this natural expression by children when it pertains to animals, but become more concerned about their participation in funeral rituals when they apply to humans. Surely here there is more need for us to allow them to see that human life is also sacred and that we can acknowledge our feelings about the worth of that life in this final ceremony – even if the child is curious about the process.

Another important and perhaps often forgotten or ignored function of the funeral ritual is that it marks the beginning of the bereaved's social recognition as a transformed individual: that is to say, the ceremony is the first public acknowledgement that the bereaved will now exist in a relation separate from the deceased, at least in a social context. The wife becomes the widow; the children become fatherless; the parents apparently are no longer parents. All concerned need to have recognition of the past and now physically ended relationship so that they are able to work out their new position in society where they now appear 'without'. The relationship with the deceased has not ended for the bereaved, but must now be different. Part of the function of the funeral is to begin this process of allowing the bereaved permission to have a new relationship with the one who is now dead.

Thought should be given to how children in school might wish to be considered if they have lost their mother. When cards are being made for Mother's Day, do we bear in mind that this is a child with no mother and therefore carefully and gently avoid the topic, or do we acknowledge mother and help the child to make a card if she wishes and to think about what she will then do with the card?

In a sense the funeral is the first public acknowledgement, but only the first part of the ceremony of memorialization. For children to be able to attend or participate in funerals, they need to be aware of what a funeral is. A simple explanation can be given. It is possible to explain even to very young children that when somebody dies we have a ceremony both to say thank you for their life and to show how much we love and miss the person. People get together to show how important the person was to them. We can explain that we choose songs and hymns that mean a lot to us or to the person who has died and say some words that have importance in the same way. We can also explain that the dead person will be in a coffin with us throughout the service because we are saying goodbye, but the person cannot hear what we say. We have them with us in the service because we want to say the things that matter in their presence before either we leave them in a grave, if they are to be buried, or before their body is burned by cremation.

It is important that the child should understand the body is no longer sentient, which may require more explanation. The child may ask, 'Won't it hurt?' 'Will they be cold?' or similar questions. We should be ready to answer these questions so the child can make sense of the process. If a family pet has died it is easy to refer back to that: 'We were sad when Fluffy died and we put her in a box and dug a hole for her and buried her in the garden. We cried because we were sad that she was dead but we made a nice grave with flowers so we would remember her.'

Often the questions children need to ask about funerals may be too difficult for us to answer if we are suffering from the loss ourselves, but if we can incorporate this information into the normal learning process and address it as it occurs naturally, then it can be a more factual and simple task. If the children have information, then they can begin to make sense of a situation. If something appears to be kept mysterious and the children are given the impression that it is wrong to ask about it, then they are left to work out their own explanations – and this may be much more disturbing than any fact about funerals could ever be.

So what additional information do we need to tell children about funerals so that they can understand not only the significance of the event in sociological terms, but also in terms of what actually happens?

How the body is prepared

Whether there is to be a burial or a cremation, there are perhaps some questions about the preparation of the body once it is dead which may need to be explained to the child, particularly as this will often have occurred outside the family home. Even where death occurs at home, the body is often removed by an undertaker and never seen again except, we assume, in the coffin at the funeral service, and then not actually seen. If we consider that the person who has died is someone about whom we care a great deal, then surely it is important that we can explain what is to happen to them and why we have allowed a stranger to take them away.

Although different religious, cultural and legal requirements may impact on the actual facts of what happens to a body, we can begin to explain that there are certain things which must happen as a mark of caring to all bodies once they are dead. So we can explain that because the person is dead and in a few hours their body will begin to go stiff, it is looked after in a way so that it will not look strange as this process sets in. This will involve closing the eyelids, supporting the jaw and sometimes arranging the body into a normal lying down position. We can also explain that the body is washed to make sure it is clean. Sometimes fluids are emanated from the body and we still want the person to be cared for even though they can no longer feel or see how they look.

Embalming

Children may assume that all bodies are embalmed, as they will have an awareness of this process from history lessons. We can explain that this does not always happen, particularly where people are buried or cremated soon after death, but that sometimes it is carried out to help the person appear a little more like they did in life so that we can look at the body. We might even mention notable people who have been embalmed and who are displayed publicly for people to visit so they can say goodbye to them: Lenin and Mao Tse-tung being two notable examples. It may be relevant here to mention the details of how bodies are embalmed, particularly if children are aware of the practices of the ancient Egyptians.

Bodies that are embalmed are first drained of blood by inserting a tube into an artery. Then a preserving fluid is put in its place, usually formalin based, which helps to fill out the body. Embalming solution is also put into the chest cavity and into the other organs of the body. The face will also be treated and then the hair, eyebrows and beard are trimmed. Make-up may be used on the face. This may seem somewhat bizarre to consider since as adults we tend not to think about such practices, but put in the context of an overall picture this is merely detail and not frightening or morbid.

Burial

Then it is important to think about what happens next: either the body is buried in the ground or it is cremated. Usually the body will be in a coffin, although there is no requirement for this to be the case. Some people choose to have the body laid in the ground in a simple body bag. In some religions a coffin is not used and the body is laid on a pallet and covered in a white sheet before being put in the ground.

When the body is buried it is lowered into the ground and covered with earth. Tombstones are often placed over the spot where the person is buried, but some people choose not to do this and there is only a small mound of earth to mark the grave.

Cremation

When a body is cremated it is taken to a crematorium and put into a cremator or furnace where it is burned at very high temperatures. The remains are then ground up in another machine to make the ashes. At this point any gold jewellery that was on the body will be removed and buried in a special and secret part of the cemetery unless the relatives ask for it. If the person had hip replacements or metal implants other than a pacemaker (which must be removed before cremation), these are not burned but will be removed by magnets in the final process. Usually the remains of an adult will weigh about two kilos (or five lbs). Bodies to be cremated are often in a coffin, but this also depends on the choice of the relatives.

I have had it suggested to me that discussing or explaining about cremation is more distressing than to talk of burial. This should not be the case where the child has understood that the body is no longer sentient, or at least is allowed to ask questions about whether it hurts to be burned, and so on. It can be quite useful to explain that there are lots of rules surrounding the permission to cremate, which make sure that even the most lurid thoughts about being burned alive can be reassured.

In Britain about 70 per cent of all disposals are by cremation so we might expect children to have heard about it, even if they do not understand what it means. In the USA cremation is less common and there are differences about attitudes towards it which are dependent on religious belief. However, explanation will be helpful to overcome fears and fantasies which can often be far worse than the reality. As with all other issues in relation to talking about death, sensitivity and honesty are the best rules we can follow.

Key points

- Legal aspects of a funeral
- Social meaning and function of a funeral
- How the body is prepared
- Embalming
- Burial
- Cremation

Chapter Eight

Cross-cultural issues

Funeral and mourning rites

In this chapter we consider the different practices and beliefs about death and burial in some of the major religions. This will be a contemporary study rather than one looking at historical practices, which will be examined in Chapters 9 and 10 when we consider the teaching of death in history lessons.

Judaism

It is customary within the Jewish faith to be buried as soon as possible after death, preferably within 24 hours. Jews do not permit cremation, so a prompt burial is not usually held up by any bureaucratic problems.

When the body is laid out, the hands should be unclenched and the feet left in a normal position. The eyes are closed, as is the jaw, and the body is covered with a white sheet. Usually the body should not be left unattended.

Although Jews believe that the body will rise again at the final judgement, death is in a sense not important. Living a good life on earth matters more. So although there are rituals surrounding death, there is also a complex sense in which death is both unimportant and of great significance as one is ready for the final judgement. The Jews have prescribed mourning rituals which divide into four stages:

1. *Aninum*: from death to the burial.

2. *Sheloshim*: 30 days from the day of burial – the first seven days are known as *shivah*.

3. The year following the death.

4. *Yahrzeit*: a perpetual remembrance of loved ones in special services.

Jewish funerals usually take place as quickly as possible after death and during this period the bereaved are known as *onen*. The fact that they are in great pain and shock is recognized within the faith and they are left alone with their grief at this stage. Friends are not expected to offer condolences until after the funeral, and indeed should not do so until the family leaves the ceremony, when they may utter the traditional words of comfort: 'May the Lord comfort you among all the other mourners of Zion and Jerusalem.'

At the funeral open expressions of grief are encouraged. Afterwards the closest family member is not left unattended for the next seven days. They undergo a state called *shivah*, which means seven. On returning from the funeral they will light a shivah candle which burns for seven days – it serves as a mark of respect for the dead. For seven days the bereaved will mourn. They may not cook, clean or do any work and they may not go out. Traditionally, mirrors will be covered with a cloth. The family of the bereaved will sit on low stools. They will not wear leather shoes or bathe (except for hygiene purposes). They must not shave, wear make-up or new clothes. All of these prohibitions are to show a retirement from worldly pursuits because the bereaved will not go out for the next seven days.

The period is divided in two where the first three days are of the deepest mourning and expected to be kept by all Jews. The next four days continue the mourning, but are not required to be kept if circumstances make this difficult. Friends must come to the house to comfort them and to provide food. The only thing that should be brought to the house at this time is a gift of food as it relieves the bereaved of worldly duties. Those coming to the house must not speak until the bereaved person begins the conversation and they must be guided by them. Often they will wash their hands as they enter the house, although this custom is not always kept nowadays. They will also recite a prayer for the dead called the *kaddish* – a prayer of remembrance which is said three times a day, usually by the eldest son. During this time the bereaved is not alone but would expect the support of friends.

After seven days the bereaved may return to some normality. Sometimes this period is marked by walking around the outside of the house. Although it is permitted to return to work after the shivah, normal life does not resume entirely and for the next 23 days of the sheloshim there is a requirement to continue to recite the kaddish three times a day. Parties, sporting events and cinema may not be attended. Orthodox Jews may not visit the grave during this period, but some reform Jews will go to the grave at the end of the shivah.

On the first anniversary of the death, the *yahrzeit*, a kaddish is said in memory of the loved one and this will occur each year on the anniversary of their death. Sometimes people will leave a pebble on the tombstone of the deceased to show that they have visited them and that they are remembered.

Hinduism

In the Hindu faith, death is never seen as a matter of great moment in the sense that it is part of a long sequence of *samsara* (rebirth). So for Hindus this is only one of many deaths and rebirths which will occur to an individual, but the moment of death has an importance as the soul of the deceased can help and be helped at this point.

For Hindus it is important that death should be allowed to occur at home if at all possible. After death members of the family wash the body and prepare it for cremation, which should take place within 24 hours of death. The ashes should be scattered in a flowing river, preferably the Ganges which is the most sacred river. During the first week following the death, readings from the holy books will take place in the home. Rituals that occur in this first ten days are called *nava-saddhras* or new and they are to help the soul (now called a *preta*) find a new body. The family must remain indoors for 10 to 13 days of mourning when they will be relieved of outside matters which will be dealt with by friends and other relatives. After the eleventh day the rituals change as the preta has now found a new location. Sometimes the *misra-saddhras* will be said for a whole year, but often they are now condensed into a single day.

Where death is anticipated, the person may be comforted by readings from holy books or the Bhagavad Ghita. They may prefer to lie on the floor to be nearer mother earth. Sometimes the family will ask the Hindu priest to tie a sacred thread (*yagyopavit*) around the wrist of the dying person as a blessing. They may wish to sprinkle holy water from the Ganges or place a sacred tulsi leaf or drops of ghee in the patient's mouth. Some relatives may want to bring clothes and money for the patient to touch, before they are distributed to the needy. Hindus believe that bodily death is not necessarily the end of life. They believe in rebirth (sometimes misinterpreted as reincarnation). The life one has lived will have an impact on how one is reborn. A virtuous and truthful life will allow the *atman* (eternal soul) to achieve *dharma*, which is the release, from the cycle of death and rebirth. This is the highest state possible.

Islam

There are important rituals that must be observed by Muslims concerning the dead. Normally the body of a dying person should be turned so that the head is facing Mecca (east). Other Muslims, preferably the family, should comfort the dying by saying prayers and reciting passages from the Koran for the peace of the soul. After death, the body should not be touched by non-Muslims because the body is the property of Allah.

Muslims, usually the sons of the deceased, carry out the washing and preparation of the body. Often the washing is done by the graveside, but this is not always possible so many mosques have a special section where this can be carried out. After the body has been washed, it is dressed in a white shroud called a *kaffon*. Prayers are then said while the body is being washed. The funeral prayer *Salat Al-Janazah* is required to be said wherever the body is washed. The body should be buried within 24 hours of death in a Muslim cemetery. This can cause difficulties in Britain due to the bureaucratic requirements of certification. Although there are some Muslim burial grounds in England they are not widespread, so Muslims may choose an appropriate site rather than a Christian burial ground.

The grave must be dug so that it is aligned with Mecca. When the body is placed within it the head will be at the east end facing towards Mecca. The body is not usually buried inside a coffin, but put into the grave in white cloth. The grave should be raised between four or twelve inches from the ground to prevent anyone from walking on it as this is strictly forbidden. Only one body may ever be laid in a grave and only a simple headstone, if any, is required.

The anniversary of the death is commemorated in the family by the giving of alms because the living must undertake the obligations which the dead person is no longer able to fulfil.

Sikhism

Sikh people are always cremated and their ashes scattered in running water, the Ganges if possible. Although the washing and preparation of the body may be carried out by the family, there is no prohibition on non-Sikhs carrying out such offices. Mourning varies in length. A long and full life with many offspring and grandchildren may be a cause for celebration, while premature death will call for a period of full mourning.

The body is prepared for the funeral by clothing it in clean clothes with the five symbols of the Sikh brotherhood, the khalsa, and then placing it on a wooden frame. There will usually be a procession to the crematorium which is of great importance – on foot or more commonly in the west by car. Hymns will be sung during the procession, but no wailing or beating of breasts is permitted as death is seen as the natural end for every person. When the body has arrived at the place of cremation the kirtan sohila is recited. A general prayer is then said which seeks a blessing for the departed.

Normally the nearest relation lights the funeral pyre, although it may not be permitted in some crematoria for the public to be very involved with this part of the process. Women who attend the funeral must wear a white head covering. On death Sikhs hope to reach unity with God through a cycle of death and rebirth and so the body of the dead person is of less importance than their soul.

After the funeral the family will return home and generally they bathe and start a reading of the scriptures called a *Sadharan Path*, which is for the benefit of the dead and their family. This should be completed in nine days and on the tenth day friends and family gather for the *bhog* ceremony. Here hymns are sung and the last five pages of Sri Granth Sahib are read. Finally *ramkali sadd* is recited for the benefit of the family of the deceased. Sometimes free food, *langar*, is distributed and presents given to the grandchildren. Donations to charities will be announced.

It may also be that another small ceremony is held on this occasion to mark a new head of the family. This is *dastar-bandi* or turban tying. The eldest son is ceremoniously given a turban to show that he is now the new head of the family and responsible for the care of the children and other dependants.

Christianity

Roman Catholics

The funeral rites celebrated in the Roman Catholic Church are to offer praise, worship and thanksgiving to God for the gift of the person's life, which, it is believed, has now returned to its creator. The Church commends the dead person to God and pleads for the forgiveness of sins. It also gives comfort and hope to the living.

The Roman Catholic ceremony is divided into three parts: the vigil, the eucharist and the committal.

During the vigil, which may take place in the home of the bereaved or in the parish church, the Christian community offers prayers and consolation to the family of the bereaved. The word of God is read and prayers of intercession are made. The rosary is often said at this time as it is felt to give hope at a time of sorrow.

The celebration of the eucharist at the funeral is to show the expression of faith that death is not the end of life, nor the end of God's love. It expresses the hope of resurrection of the dead. The coffin will be placed in the church for this ceremony and will be covered with the pall.

The committal is said at the place of burial where the body is placed to rest. It is to express the hope that the deceased will experience the glory of the resurrection. Normally, Roman Catholics are not cremated but prefer burial, not only because this was the manner of Christ's own burial, but also out of respect for the body and belief in the resurrection – which is bodily resurrection unlike some of the other faiths. Cremation is permitted under some circumstances, but the ashes may not be scattered and should always be buried in consecrated ground.

The Society of Friends (Quakers)

The Quakers believe that the end of bodily life is not the end of life, but that the person will go from this world to be with God. The emphasis on eternal life is less pronounced as Quakers feel it is important to live to their best every day on earth. The emphasis on bodily resurrection is not as strong as with the Roman Catholics and there is no prohibition on cremation. This is often the preferred method of disposal, because it is cheaper and simpler. Simple burials do occur, but elaborate headstones are not used and if a headstone is made it will simply state the name and dates on it.

Usually the cremation ceremony will be attended only by the family and this will be followed by a memorial at which the body is not present. The memorial is an unstructured service which may contain poems, readings or remembrances of the deceased. This service may contain both tears and laughter, the main idea being memorial not just to focus on the individual but on the larger community. All Quaker ceremonies are simple. The public display of grief is not important therefore, and though connection to others may be considered in the memorial overt displays of grief are not deemed appropriate.

Buddhism

There are several different forms of Buddhism, but we shall consider here the Chinese tradition and how they observe funeral rites. Buddhists cremate their dead, but there is no need for this to be done quickly after death. Indeed, sometimes the ceremony is delayed either to allow family to return from a distance or to allow prayers for the soul of the deceased to be said to help them in their next life.

In the Chinese tradition there are two forms of funeral rite. In the first, the ceremony lasts over 49 days, of which the first seven are the most important. Prayers are said every seven days for the 49 days if the family can afford it. If they are too poor, these will just be said for the first three or seven days. Daughters usually carry the cost of the funeral expenses within this tradition. The head of the family (male) should be at all the prayers, but at least the first two. The head of the family should also be at the cremation.

In the second tradition, the prayer ceremony is held every ten days – with an initial ceremony and then three periods of ten days following the cremation. After 100 days a final prayer ceremony is held, but this tends to be optional.

Buddhists believe that death occurs and then the person will be reborn. Between the death and rebirth there is a period called *antarabhava*. This is an important time when it is possible to influence the form in which the rebirth will take place. The prayers and ceremonies assist a favourable rebirth. Buddhists believe that death is suffering, but that this is relieved by rebirth, so there is a sort of resignation about the funeral ceremony.

When someone is dying, an effort is made to get the person to concentrate on the scriptures if they can, or to whisper four sounds into the ear of the dying so that the last thoughts are directed towards Buddha. This will bring good things to the deceased in their new existence.

After death a bathing ceremony takes place in which friends and relatives pour water over one hand of the deceased. The body is then placed in a coffin, surrounded by wreaths, candles and incense. Sometimes if the cremation is to be delayed a priest will come to say prayers and attach a broad ribbon to the coffin which the priest holds. This is called a *bhusa yong*. Its purpose is to connect the deceased directly with the prayers so that they may help as meritorious acts for the rebirth. Food given to the priests is considered to be meritorious. The accompanying of the dead to the funeral ceremony is also a meritorious act. After cremation, the ashes are collected and kept in an urn. In the east it is not uncommon for bodies to be preserved in the temple for a year or more in order to show love for the deceased and to perform religious rites for their benefit.

Key points

Funeral and mourning rituals

- Judaism
- Hinduism
- Islam
- Sikhism
- Christianity
- Buddhism

Chapter Nine

The process of grieving
in children explained

In this chapter we examine how children grieve with reference to how this occurs at different developmental stages. We consider how their concept of death is different at each stage and how attachment theory can help us understand the concept of loss. We shall think about how this will assist us in talking to children about the death, helping them to cope with loss and appropriate ways in which to do this.

Adult assumptions about children's grief

It was long thought that children did not grieve in the same way as adults, if at all. This assumption allowed adults who were themselves coping with the loss of a loved to feel reassured that children would be coping all right on their own as they did not feel the loss in the same way as the adult. Children sometimes display an apparent lack of 'natural' emotional reaction to situations that the adults think should arouse deep feeling. The child may be considered heartless, not caring or not affected. We are all aware of people commenting in this sort of way about children who have suffered a bereavement saying things like 'I don't think they remember' or 'She doesn't seem to be too upset'. But these comments belie the fact that mourning is occurring for the child: children do remember people and they do grieve, although it is not always manifested in a way which adults recognize as grief.

How children grieve

A child does not grieve in a linear way and go through a process that can be tracked easily. The child is going through a process, but it is one which the child may repeat, having apparently mastered one level of coping, only to return to it at a later date. This is because children are also developing cognitively and will become aware of the significance of events in different ways as they mature. It may be because the adults feel that children need to be shielded from the thought of death and it is often thought that children do not think about death and should be protected from it.

Bowlby (1981) offers us four phases of mourning that he says apply to both children and adults. The phases are not clear cut in the sense that one must go through them in a particular order. An individual may oscillate for a time back and forth between any two of them. Yet there is an overall sequence that can be discerned over time which can be weeks or months. The four phases are as follows: numbing; yearning; disorganization and despair; reorganization.

Numbing

This usually lasts from a few hours to a few weeks and may be interrupted by outbursts of intense distress or anger. This is the state in which we often find ourselves when told something which is just too much to absorb initially. I am sure we have all experienced situations when our immediate reaction to some news is to not believe it. This is a healthy initial response and a psychic defence mechanism. The function of the initial disbelief and numbing is to give us time to assimilate new information and to reorganize our cognitive map in order to set the new information within it, so that we can at least begin to try to make sense of it. There is some evidence that without the initial numbing and an apparent immediate acceptance of the news, the prognosis for grieving in a healthy way is poor.

Yearning

The phase of yearning and searching for the loved one can last some months or years. In this phase we seek to recover the lost person, perhaps in concrete ways or in memory. Those who have been bereaved will be aware of perhaps being worried or distressed when they realize that they cannot call to mind the loved one's face or their voice. Sometimes this would cause the bereaved to seek things that would trigger these memories in order to not lose the loved one over again. This happens not only with the death of a loved one, but is also common when we leave our loved ones for any prolonged length of time. In this stage it is also not uncommon either to see the loved one or to experience their presence in a very real way. Conversations are often held out loud or in the head and this can be reassuring for the bereaved person.

Disorganization and despair

There is loss of hope and a sense that future life is uncertain and of no significance. Life no longer makes sense and has no meaning. There is a feeling of dissociation with a world that is continuing as if nothing has changed. Yet for the bereaved person the world no longer exists in a way that makes sense or has any purpose. In his play about C.S. Lewis, Nicholson (1989) considers Lewis's reaction to the death of his wife Joy. On his first dinner with colleagues, Harrington says to him: 'Life must go on.' Lewis replies: 'I don't know that it must. But it certainly does.'

I think this reflects the state of disorganization and despair very clearly. There is no point. There may be thoughts of suicide at this time or a rather less active sense of wanting to be dead to be with the loved one. There seems to be no point in investing in the future. Eating may become a chore, as may many other ordinary activities. This is a depressive state.

Reorganization

There is a readiness to reinvest in life and to begin new relationships. This is not forgetting or pulling oneself together. This is a state of having accepted life as it now is and allowing oneself to live in the present and the future in a changed way.

At times of stress it may be that a former phase is revisited. A child who appears to have begun to reinvest in life may be distressed and feel hopeless if they suffer another loss and may need time to assimilate it before they can move forward again.

Freud suggested that children only think of death in terms of a journey, as if to suggest that this implies that they do not have any real concept of what death may mean. But this is not so very different from how adults think of death. Susan Isaacs (1930) observed adults' reactions to children's thoughts about death and noted: 'It has not been considered desirable that children should take any interest in…the facts of death' (p.33).

The wish that children should not think about death arises from the adult's own fear of it and is not founded on objective observation of children. Bowlby has argued that children do mourn as much as adults and has offered a model for the stages through which children go to help us understand their unique process of grieving.

> The mourning responses that are commonly seen in infancy and early childhood bear many of the features which are the hallmark of pathological mourning in the adult. (Bowlby 1963, p.504)

Developmental stages and grief

What do we need to understand about the child's concept of death? First, it is important to establish what the child is likely to be able to conceptualize in terms of permanence. Although there may be some controversy about the usefulness and accuracy of developmental stages, they are a useful tool to have as a guideline against which we can measure the likely ability of a child to understand certain concepts.

It is suggested by Piaget (1954) that not until the last stage of development (formal operations) does a child have a fully formed concept of death as irreversible and final. Some understanding that death is permanent will have been gained at the stage of concrete operations and therefore it is possible for a child of eight to understand death as final.

However, it has been argued by others (Nagy 1948; Worden 1989) that children as young as two have the capacity to understand that death is significantly different from life as a state. We can see this from their questioning and curiosity about dead plants and animals. They may poke small animals to see if they can make them move. Finding that they cannot, they will conclude that this state is not the same as sleep from which they can arouse creatures (as many a family pet will be aware).

The work of Sylvia Anthony (1940) shows very clearly the interest that children naturally display in death.

Piaget (1954) considers the following to be the child's concept of death at each stage.

Sensory-motor stage

CHILD'S CONCEPT OF DEATH: ALL GONE

This stage lasts from birth to two years of age. If the child cannot see something, it does not exist. From about six months the child begins to develop the concept that some things do exist, even when the child cannot see them.

Preoperational stage

CHILD'S CONCEPT OF DEATH: MAGICAL, EGOCENTRIC AND CAUSAL

This stage lasts from two to seven years of age. The child thinks of death as temporary and partial. Death is reversible and the child considers it is possible to revive the body by food and warmth. The child thinks that its own thoughts or actions could cause death. This is magical thinking.

Concrete operational stage

CHILD'S CONCEPT OF DEATH: CURIOUS AND REALISTIC

This stage lasts from 7 to 12 years of age. Children are curious about birth, death and sex. They are very interested in the details of death. They can conceptualize that all bodily functions cease. They understand that dead people can't breathe, smell, move, hear or see. They can express logical thoughts and fears about death. Children think of death in terms of specific, concrete, observable terms. When someone has died they may ask, 'Who killed him?'

Formal operational stage

ADOLESCENT'S CONCEPT OF DEATH: SELF-ABSORBED

This stage is from 13 years of age upwards. Adolescents understand mortality and death as a natural process. Death seems remote and something they can control. The denial of their own death is strong. Usually they feel it happens to the old and very sick.

We can compare Piaget's stages to those that Maria Nagy (1948) believes apply.

- *Stage 1: 3 to 5 years old.* Death is temporary, a continuation of life, being asleep. It is neither universal nor personal.

- *Stage 2: 5 to 9 years old.* Death is final, personified, neither universal nor personal. Death can be eluded.

- *Stage 3: 9 years old upwards.* Death is final, personal and universal.

There are some similarities between the two models, although Nagy (1948) believes that children come to a fuller understanding of death at a much earlier age than does Piaget (1954). What is important for us to notice is that children do think about death from a very early age. They are therefore affected by it and need to make some sense of it insofar as they are capable. Infants may not have a fully formed concept of death but they are beginning to make sense of things being present and not there. They can understand loss as it applies to them, so it is useful to consider attachment formation in order to see how young children can experience real pain in loss even though we may not realize that they are grieving.

Attachment theory

It is useful to have some understanding of attachment theory in order better to understand why a loss might have a greater impact than might be expected if the relationship is not clear to the adult.

What we see in mourning is a longing to regain the lost person. There may be an initial lack of acceptance that the loved one is in fact dead (denial) and a desire for them to return. There will be times when the bereaved person feels an overwhelming sense that the loved one is still present. This may include a psychological sense of their presence or even a visual perception of their presence. The desire to keep the loved one close is enhanced by keeping significant objects nearby or looking at photographs. This is not abnormal in the first few months; nor indeed is it abnormal to 'see' the loved one. The desire to recover the loved one is a natural response, particularly when there has been a good attachment in the past. It refers us back to a very early stage of development where the infant seeks the proximity of the 'mother figure' by crying to elicit a protective reaction. As the infant develops, if the response has been forthcoming the infant is able to internalize the 'mother figure' so that the reassurance of her presence can be felt even when she is absent for short periods. We can see the distress displayed when the child is not reassured of the parent's return. Robertson (1953) wrote about this reaction from observations made in the early 1950s:

> If a child is taken from his mother's care at this age (18–24 mths), when he is possessively and passionately attached to her, it is indeed as if his world has been shattered. His intense need of her is unsatisfied, and the frustration and longing may send him frantic with grief. (Robertson 1953)

When a loved one dies that reassurance does not occur as the loved one cannot return, but the desire remains for this to happen. Although we may like to feel that children forget quickly, it would seem that this is wishful thinking on the part of adults in the hope that the pain does not last long. The same studies by Robertson showed that although after a phase of protest the child does indeed become quieter, but rather than this being evidence of forgetting it would seem to be an indication that the child has moved into a phase of despair and is still as strongly attached as before.

If the attachments formed in early life are secure, this can help the child to cope with this painful and sad phase. The bereaved person is eventually able to move on to the next stage of life when they reorganize without the loved one and new attachments are possible:

> Although we know that after…a loss the acute state of mourning will subside, we also know we shall remain inconsolable and will never find a substitute. No matter what may fill the gap, even if it be filled completely, it nevertheless remains something else. And actually this is how it should be. It is the only way of perpetuating that love which we do not wish to relinquish. (Freud 1917, p.250)

The loss of the loved person gives rise not only to an intense desire for reunion, but also to anger at his or her departure, and later to some degree of detachment. This can cause an ambivalent reaction in that there is a desire to be comforted, but a rejection of those who offer help as the helper is not the loved one.

The process of attachment can be likened to falling in love. Maintaining the bond is like loving someone and consequently losing that person is like grieving over someone. The threat of loss arouses anxiety and actual loss causes sorrow. In some situations the loss can cause anger. If the bond is maintained there is an experience of security and the renewal of that bond will cause joy. The healthy development of early attachments is an indicator of how the individual will cope with loss of any sort, but it is also important to note how the process of grieving is one with which we are all familiar since it is part of our early experience in the development of early attachment.

Although there are situations where grief may be complicated and become what is termed 'abnormal grieving', it is usual for any grieving to be painful and to take time to recover from.

The mourning process can thus be likened to the healing stages that follow a severe wound or burn. In this analogy we should bear in mind that the time scale for healing will vary with each individual, depending on a variety of differing circumstances. Even when the wound has healed there may still be some impairment of function or sign of something being slightly different from before. So it is with mourning. It takes time to be able to make new relationships and to leave the old one and it may be that forming new relationships remains a difficult thing to do. There may be a lack of trust or a fear of commitment as we now realize more fully that people leave us. Investment in a new relationship will inevitably have risks.

Talking to children who are grieving

Talking to anyone who has suffered bereavement is never easy. We feel embarrassed and do not know what to say. We are concerned not to say the wrong thing. Sometimes we are worried that we will upset the person and make them feel worse, so often we avoid them, or at best avoid talking about the bereavement.

There are some important points to bear in mind when dealing with children who have suffered bereavement. The most important factor is that the loss itself is probably the greatest pain which they can suffer and you can neither make it go away nor make it worse by talking openly. If you avoid talking about the fact that the child has lost a loved one, you deny the significance of the relationship and demonstrate that it is not important, thereby increasing the child's distress. We have to try to remember whose embarrassment we are dealing with – theirs or our own. The chances are that it is we who feel embarrassed and uncertain. If we do not know what to say, then perhaps we should admit it. Then at least we are acknowledging that something important has happened, but we are not sure how to deal with it. Isn't this often how it is?

As adults we are used to being in charge, able to cope and knowing what to do. We expect to be able to ease painful situations for children, but in this circumstance we cannot. No matter what we say, we cannot bring people back from the dead. We cannot make it better, but maybe we can try to not make it worse. It is important for adults to feel comfortable with the child's pain if they are to be of any help to the child.

Winnicott (1986) has a concept which he calls 'holding'. This refers to the psychological process within therapy where the therapist listens to the client and accepts whatever is said. It is a sharing with another where the other is able to hold on to the painful thoughts and words and not be disgusted or frightened by them. This is a form of psychological hand holding where nothing else can be said or done, but the fact of the human contact is in itself reassuring and helpful. For adults it is distressing to be in a position where they feel unable to help as they are usually the ones to whom children to turn to ease their pain. However, it is possible to acknowledge the pain and the distress and help the child to understand the reality of what has happened.

Language

The language used when talking to children about death is important. Although we may use figures of speech to help our general conversations so that we do not use the words dead and dying, we need to be aware of the child's literal turn of mind. To try to comfort children with phrases such as 'grandma has gone to sleep' or 'she has gone to live with the angels' will actually cause greater distress than the truth that grandma is dead and cannot come back to see us again. It is not uncommon for 'going to sleep' to be used as a euphemism for death, but the effect on a small child is to cause them severe anxieties about going to sleep at all. If grandma has 'gone to live with the angels' then she can come back again because one trip is much like any other to a child. Another thought that occurs if this is said is that a trip to see the angels might appeal greatly to the child and they may become anxious to join granny, thus causing other difficulties. Unless told otherwise, a child will naturally assume that heaven is much like any other distant place and that a return is only a matter of time.

If we use the phrase 'lost' then we have to consider that children will have experience of things being lost or even of having been lost themselves. Often the lost thing is found, or at least we make sure that we look for it. It may cause reasonable anger that someone should get themselves lost or be allowed to be mislaid in such a careless way. This is not reassuring. When we consider the types of euphemisms we commonly use to explain to children that someone has died, we rapidly become aware that they are not at all helpful and very confusing.

Even when talking about pets we often avoid the truth that the animal has become too sick or too old and is now dead. A friend told me that it was not until he was in his thirties that his mother told him that when they moved his much loved dog had not gone to live on a farm but had been taken to the vet to be put down. He was genuinely upset to have believed that although the dog could not come to live in their new home it was happily running about and one day he might even be able to visit it on the farm. The child given this type of explanation for a pet or a person begins to wonder why they don't want to live with them anymore and also assumes that a return is possible and so cannot move on from that hope.

Make the loss real

There are two crucial items of information that a child needs to know: first, the dead person will never return; second, the body is to be buried in the ground or burned to ashes. It is hard to say such words to children, but unless they know these things they will not and cannot grieve, as they believe they are suffering only a temporary loss. The child will inevitably want to ask questions about the body, such as who will feed it, will it hurt if people walk over the ground where it is buried or won't it be painful to be put into a big fire. Clearly the child needs also to understand that the body once dead is no longer sentient, that it will feel no pain, cold, hunger, and so on. It is also important that the child is told that being dead is not at all like being asleep. When we go to sleep our bodies continue to function, our hearts still beat, we breathe, and so on. When we die, from whatever cause, the heart stops beating, the brain no longer functions and so all the other parts of the body stop doing their work as well. Death is a different state from life and it is normal and not frightening, although the circumstances of the death may be distressing and painful.

The first task of mourning is to accept the reality of the loss. We can only help the child to do this by being open and honest. If we avoid the truth then we allow for confusion and do not give the child permission to grieve because we have not said that there has been a real loss. We are not being kind by not telling the truth; it will not make things easier. We need to do this within the context of the child's cognitive ability to understand the concept of death. This may mean that we have to explain the same facts over and over again. It is important to allow the child the time to assimilate this new information and not to become impatient or consider them morbid if they frequently want to know what happens to the body once it is dead. Bowlby (1981) talks about this need to allow time for cognitive mastery. It is important to bear in mind that children are developing emotionally and cognitively. Therefore although they may have been given information straight away, they may seek to clarify and question at a later date as their capacity to understand changes. Consider the child's normal desire for repetition of well-known events, such as 'Tell me what it was like when I came out of your tummy'. This may be a frequently told story, but one that the child finds useful to hear repeated as it fits them into the world and helps them understand how they came to be.

It is also a common and normal reaction to any traumatic event to need to repeat the situation in order to assimilate it into one's own cognitive map. This is what we need to do if, for example, we have even a minor car accident. We retell the event and consider the possible outcomes in order to gain some sort of mastery over it. Trauma debriefing is based on the principle of this universal need. So when we say that we need to talk about a death it is important for us to bear this in mind that without the facility to talk about the event there can be no real understanding and therefore the possibility of moving on is severely restricted.

Although it may be felt that the subject of death should be avoided as too distressing for a child, this will not help but only produce the opposite effect from that intended. Not mentioning it gives the message that this is something which adults don't like to talk about. The reasons for this will be constructed by the child in terms of being something bad, naughty or for which they may be to blame. They will certainly learn that death is not to be talked about and therefore they will learn to be silent. They may learn not to cry as all the adults are trying to refrain from crying in their presence. Don't we normally cry when something sad happens? So what message does the child learn here? Something sad has happened and no one is to cry. They may even be told that they have to be brave and good for mummy now. So was the child neither brave nor good before? Is that why the person died?

We can inadvertently set up all sorts of answers to questions that were never asked. The child seeks to make sense of the event, so if we cannot explain they will make some sense of it themselves. This is a natural thing which we all do. We try to make sense of events we cannot understand in order to help us cope. It is difficult to make sense of some deaths. If an old person dies we can perhaps feel at ease with this because we can talk about the natural wearing out of the body and how this fits into a natural life cycle. With deaths that come out of order, as with sudden death, infant death, suicide or accidents, it becomes harder for us to explain why the person had to die. The best we can do is to tell the truth and say we do not know. Adults do not need to know everything. They can say they don't know.

It is important to answer the question that has been asked. By this I mean that because of our anxiety about how to answer the difficult questions we may assume that the child is seeking information we are anxious about. If the child says 'Where do you go when you are dead?' this is not necessarily a request for a metaphysical answer. It might mean does the person stay at home or go to hospital or do they go straight to the cemetery. It is essential to check out what is being asked as we may overcomplicate the task we have to do through our own anxieties.

Emotional coping

At a time of bereavement adults are often in the difficult position of not only having to cope with their own loss, but also with that of the child. It is natural to want to protect the child and to seem strong for them in order to reassure that all will be well. But there is a danger in hiding our own adult grief too carefully in that it can give the wrong message to the child by not providing strength and reassurance, but creating a taboo subject. To help stimulate emotional coping it is important that the child feels death and dying are subjects which can be talked about openly. The dead person is someone who can be remembered and spoken of with both happy and sad memories. This will ease the child's fear of death, because they will see that the adults around them can cope or at least are not paralysed and frightened by what has happened. Adults do not need to conceal their own sadness about the loss. Indeed it is reassuring and helpful to see that adults are also sad and upset when someone important to them has died. We can model good grieving for children in the same way that we model other behaviours.

Common behaviours in the grieving child

It is possible to create a list of how a child may react to grief, but inevitably the list will be incomplete. However, what we need to be aware of is the fact that a significant event has occurred in the child's life and it is important that we acknowledge it. There may be changes in behaviour such as becoming withdrawn or loud and naughty. Some children become anxious and unable to accept reassurance from adults, needing physical proximity to someone they trust. This may mean that the child develops a false maturity and tries to parent others.

A child who has previously been outgoing and confident may become clingy and even school phobic. So we can see that one child may be rejecting of adult attention and another may crave it. There can be some regressive behaviours such as bedwetting, thumbsucking, babytalk, needing to sleep with the light on or with the parent. Some children are anxious about the health of those around them and constantly worry that others too will die.

Clearly children need to be reassured about the likelihood of this but should also not be given false promises. With some children symptoms are physical and they display an increased number of stomach aches, headaches, weariness, tightness of the throat, and so on. Others become moody, depressed or angry. Mood changes are particularly problematic in adolescence, as it is not always clear whether they are connected to the bereavement or to developmental changes. However, the adults around the children who are coping with loss need to remain aware and be observant. It is not necessary to persuade the child to talk about their loss, but rather to acknowledge the fact of it and be available when the child does need to talk.

Dealing with bereaved children is not easy. Our own anxieties about death may prevent us from feeling comfortable with some of their questions. They present us with particular difficulties as adults since we naturally feel the need to comfort, reassure and protect them from harm. But these children are hurting in a way that we cannot ease and often they lack trust in adults as their faith in life has been shattered. The rules about helping these children are simple:

- Be honest and open.

- Don't try to make it better.

- Say you don't know if you can't answer their questions.

- Go at the child's pace.

If a child asks about cremation it is not morbid. It is no more scary or distressing to know that a body will be burned than to be put in the ground, as long as the child understands that the body can no longer feel. Going to live with angels is not necessarily a comforting thought, as the child might wonder why mummy preferred to live with the angels rather than her own child. Getting it wrong is not a problem, as long as you tell the truth, answer real questions and do not leave the child confused. There are four very simple rules to bear in mind.

- *Rule one*: Be honest. If you don't know, say so. Don't be evasive. Be clear.

- *Rule two*: Use words carefully. Don't use euphemisms.

- *Rule three*: Be prepared to answer the same question several times. The child needs time to make sense of new information.

- *Rule four.* Be aware of your own anxieties and worries. Don't feel you ought to feel comfortable with talk of death if you don't.

Key points

- Adult assumptions about children's grief
- How children grieve
- Developmental stages and grief
- Attachment theory
- Talking to children who are grieving
- Common behaviours in the grieving child

Chapter Ten

Death across the curriculum

Normalizing talk of death in the classroom

In this chapter we consider how death can be incorporated into the curriculum in a sensible and simple way. The aim is neither to describe a way of teaching about death and loss as a separate subject, nor as a part of citizenship or personal, social and health education (PSHE), but to consider how this subject area can be discussed naturally within almost all areas of the curriculum with a little imagination and creativity. It would be foolish not to acknowledge that many adults have some anxiety talking about death and loss, particularly with children, but it is hoped that by considering how the subject occurs naturally in so many areas of life we can begin to think about a useful and non-threatening way in which to introduce and tackle it.

What follows are not lesson plans as such but rather suggestions which teachers may wish to try for themselves. This is not meant to be a programme to be followed, but a way of stimulating thought about how they might embark upon this style of teaching for themselves. The list of examples is by no means exhaustive and is not intended to be. Teachers should use this merely as a guide and suit the model we offer to their own personal style of teaching. The rule we follow is that there should be a lightness of touch; death is to be picked up naturally from the subject matter already being taught. The issues surrounding death are already present within the curriculum, as they are in any life. This is a way of considering those issues and not avoiding them. Death is part of life and part of the lives of each of us, no matter the age. It is neither a prescription, nor a new subject; just an acknowledgement of information to be imparted and not avoided. It is also important to bear in mind that there will not always be answers to the questions that arise from the topic. This should be acknowledged and need not be a bar to beginning this work.

Using the National Curriculum to talk about death

Here we consider how death fits into schooling in England and Wales. This is of particular relevance from National Curriculum Key Stage 2, because by this age children will mostly understand that death is irreversible. In other areas the topics looked at can be considered in relation to the curriculum as it applies there. Death can be talked about at earlier stages or later stages with thought and consideration. Some of the examples will more easily be of use in secondary education rather than primary. By employing the examples of how one might fit the subject into a broad education programme, we hope that it will be possible to consider how this fits with education in other countries.

What follows is a selection of possible ways of introducing or discussing death in a natural and unobtrusive way within the children's curriculum. Discussion comes from the material almost spontaneously or is an obvious next step.

Consideration is given to the connections and teaching points that might be picked up from various topics and curriculum areas.

The Victorians

History, sociology, health issues, linked with news

By considering the life and reign of Queen Victoria we can look at the many changes she underwent as a person, first as a young woman who married for love, despite opposition, and then later as a mother of many children.

- What was the size of the average family in the nineteenth century?

- Why was it usual to have large families?

- Is this the case for most people nowadays in the western world? Why not?

- What legal changes occurred in the registration of births, when and why?

Next as the life of Queen Victoria progresses we come to the death of her dear husband, Prince Albert, and might consider the impact of this event on her life and how it affected her subjects as a consequence.

- What were the changes in her appearance/clothing?

- Do people wear black clothes today for mourning? When might they wear black for mourning?

- Consider the importance of the Albert memorial.

- A new fashion in jewellery occurred – wearing jet often as mourning.

- Artwork often also appeared as memento mori. Do we have this? How?

- Was the funeral of Prince Albert like anything we might be aware of nowadays? The funerals of Winston Churchill and Diana, Princess of Wales might be compared.

We may wish to consider how the preservation and display of bodies differs in different countries. The body of Victoria is not preserved and displayed anywhere, but the body of Chairman Mao is still on display in Beijing. We might even consider how Queen Elizabeth, the Queen Mother might be mourned or celebrated when she dies. Why might this be an important state occasion?

Considering some of the important events that occurred during the reign of Queen Victoria, we might start with the various wars:

- 1840 war against China and Afghanistan
- 1854–6 Crimean War
- 1857–8 Indian rebellion crushed
- 1861–5 American Civil War
- 1873 Ashanti War
- 1879 Zulu War
- 1900 Boxer rebellion.

From this broad list we can see that from almost the beginning of Queen Victoria's reign in 1837 there was not a single decade free from war in some part of the world which involved the British troops. Although the scale of public involvement in these wars would not have been as widely known as nowadays, it might be worth considering how they were reported and what people knew about them.

- Can the children think of any wars they know about?

- How did they know about them?
- Did they know if people died?
- How?

This might lead us to consider health and the improvements/breakthroughs in medicine that were occurring during the nineteenth century. This also involves a consideration of housing, factories and poverty.

The events leading up to the Anatomy Act are both gruesome and fun for young children.

- Who were the body snatchers?
- Why did they steal bodies?
- Who was more usually used for anatomy?
- Do we hang people today in this country?
- Do some countries still have capital punishment?
- Why was it important to be buried whole?
- Do we still think this?
- Can we think of any times when this hasn't happened or ways that maybe something a bit like body snatching has occurred in recent times?

Some children, particularly in secondary school, might consider events in Britain that have been in the news since the year 2000 when the removal of body parts for use in research has been a matter of public interest.

This might lead us on to think of the class differences in funeral rituals – so we can consider paupers' graves.

- How does this compare to the mass graves found in the Balkans?

Funeral coaches might be considered and the employment of mutes to walk in front of the funeral cortège. An example of this is seen in the film *Oliver* by Lionel Bart.

- Who was employed to do this job?
- Would we think of it as a career?

A local cemetery might be used to provide a useful source of information that can be incorporated into many subjects.

Rites of passage and festivals

Art, geography, history

In terms of looking at other cultures, religions and philosophies we may tend to concentrate on the happy occasions as we see them. However, in many cultures there are rituals celebrating the dead and these need not be considered morbid in any way. As we have seen in Chapter 8, many religions have quite elaborate rituals concerning grief and mourning. These should be included in any consideration of other cultures as they tell us something important about how people see the living.

Starting from an art lesson we can look at a ritual from Mexico, the Day of the Dead. First, we can study the type of images used, what colours are used and language that might be associated with these images. We can compare this to 'In sympathy' cards available in Britain and the USA and consider whether these are similar or not.

- What images are used on these cards?
- What colours are used?
- What does this tell us about how we see death in this culture?
- How is it different?

We might then go on to look at funerary art. This might have been looked at in studying the Victorian era. We can consider the elaborate tombstones often found in nineteenth century graveyards and compare them to those in more modern cemeteries.

- Have the images changed?
- Has the size of the statuary altered?

By looking at the gravestones in a local cemetery it will be possible to consider what images were used and whether they differ over time. It will be possible to check the age at which the person died and see if the images used on the gravestones of children are the same as those of older people.

- What about cemeteries in countries across the world?
- How do they differ from ones we know?
- What might this tell us about their attitudes towards death?

We might consider the French tradition of visiting family graves on 1 November, All Saints Day, which is a national holiday. On that day it is traditional to put chrysanthemums on the family graves. We have these flowers in our homes, but the French do not as they are funeral flowers. Do we have a flower we connect with funerals?

Unexpected news

Answering questions openly

Often children come into class with news about something that has happened to them at home and are keen to tell everybody about it. Sometimes the news might be about a sad or distressing event, which the child may or may not see as such. It will not be unusual to have children come into school with news that their pet has died. This can be used as an opportunity to teach about death or to consider how we deal with loss. It would be unusual if only one child had experienced loss through death, so this event can be applied helpfully for all children. We can start by asking some simple questions about the pet.

- What was the name of the pet?
- What did the pet look like?
- What colour was it?
- How old was the pet?
- How did it die?

The child may not be fully aware of the answer to the last question or they may have a detailed knowledge of the events surrounding the death of the pet. Other children might be invited (or more likely will not be able to be stopped) to share their experiences of pets dying or seeing other dead animals. A useful question to ask is about how we know it is dead. This can allow us to go on to consider how being dead is a different state from being alive, and more particularly being asleep.

- Did you see the pet when it was dead?
- What did you notice (if anything)?
- Did you touch or stroke the pet?
- How did it feel?
- Did anyone say not to touch it?
- Why do you think that was?
- What will happen to it/has happened to it?
- Is that OK for you or should we find a way of saying goodbye in class?

The teacher might feel that discussing the death of a pet is potentially risky as some children may have lost grandparents, parents or siblings and it could be distressing for them to consider these things. If the subject is addressed with care and sensitivity it will not be a problem and may indeed be a relief for the child to be able to ask questions or to understand what being dead means.

Clearly using each opportunity to have a short discussion about death when it has occurred means that the next time there is a death to talk about the children will be aware that it is OK to mention it, and we can be aware that we have a framework to refer back to.

Using this sort of event more formally as part of a science lesson can also be useful. It would probably be inappropriate immediately to turn the news item into a science lesson. However, at some point during that day or week the event can be referred to while considering the life cycle. One might talk about plants initially and make comment that animals also die. This may be all that is said or we might go on to consider what happens to the animal when it dies in terms of rigor mortis, lack of senses, lack of heat, and so on.

Using number

Maths, science, history, sociology, health

There are many interesting facts and figures associated with death which can be considered for use in a variety of ways to stimulate maths lessons and debate in a broader way. First, let us consider calculating the worth of the body (see for example *http://library.thinkquest.org/16665/worth.htm*). Here we can see what elements go into making up the body of any person. By calculating weight and height we can also work out how much of each element an individual is likely to possess, and its current market value – thus being able to calculate the worth of an individual. This gives us material for both maths and science and allows us to consider whether the actual worth of the elements can bear any relation to how we feel about the worth of an individual and why this might not be a way of working out what people are worth.

In some cases this could also lead us on to looking at how insurance agencies calculate the pay-outs for the death of an individual in different circumstances. This means looking at health statistics, probability and gender differences and so holds a wealth of interesting and useful material for teaching purposes. We can calculate the average life expectancy of the particular class being taught, which is about mean averages. It will alter slightly from the tables given for different countries in terms of distribution of gender. So the average for a class with more girls in it will be higher than one with more boys in it.

This can also be used historically to look at what the average might have been had the children been born in the early part of the twentieth century, which leads on to discussion about what changes have occurred to cause the differences in life expectancy. Again information gleaned from a cemetery can be useful for comparison of life expectancy. Where a cemetery has war graves it will be possible to use the dates of the deceased to make inferences about the enlistment of soldiers (the majority of these graves will be of young men). It may be that these graves differ between wars.

Information from gravestones will also tell us in which month a person died. We can use this information to see whether death is spread evenly across the year or if there are differences at certain times of the year. Do more people die in January than June for example? Additional calculations can be made about whether any difference applies across all age ranges or only to the elderly.

This information may also lead us to find out about public health matters. There may be a prevalence of deaths in one part of a particular year that can be traced to a cholera epidemic or a natural disaster.

We can then go on to consider how this might be different in different countries in the present day: What factors are significant here? These facts and figures increase the children's understanding of diet, nutrition, impact of war, and so on. They are clearly in no way morbid, but an interesting and novel method of teaching about the world in a real way.

Using film and the media
Science, history, art, PSHE

Children will see representations of death and dying in a variety of forms on a regular basis through cartoon images, feature films and news items on television and in the newspapers. All of these can be used in a variety of ways from PSHE to English and drama to maths and science lessons. The information and images are part of the child's experience and not something alien to them. We might begin by thinking about the way death does not occur in cartoons.

- How often does a cartoon character run into a tunnel and get flattened by a train only to appear rolled out thinly like pastry and then to shake themselves back to life again.

- How many cartoon bombs explode only to give the character hair that stands on end and a soot-covered face.

We can look at these and talk about the reality of what has actually happened to the character.

- Is that likely?
- Would he have died?
- What injuries might he have sustained?
- Would this accident have been life threatening?
- Why do we think it is funny in a cartoon?
- If it were a film would this accident be funny?
- Why/why not?

We can then compare images of death and dying in films and see how they are portrayed differently. Do people die or only certain characters? In action films usually the hero will fight against impossible odds and come out unscathed. We might consider whether this is realistic or possible. We might consider why this has to be the case and why the real or likely outcome is not shown in the film.

- In some films people do die – so what is the difference here?
- What do we learn about how death is portrayed in different ways and with different cultures?
- Is the reaction to the news of death realistic or likely?
- Do we see this?

So many films and news stories talk about death that it is unlikely that there will be a single child who has not been aware of death in the media. News reports about disasters are valuable tools and can be considered in a variety of ways. In January 2001 there was an earthquake in El Salvador causing landslides that destroyed housing and trapped many people. This is not an uncommon event to hear about, although in Europe there are very few earthquakes. What is it that causes the deaths – falling buildings, falling into gaping holes in the ground (as often shown in disaster movies) or is it more likely to be due to asphyxiation after being trapped under mud or debris for days?

Here we can consider the geography of where these types of events are most likely to occur, consider the type of buildings – if they differ in any way from those we are used to. We can consider how predictions about the next earthquake are made and whether people prepare for them. We might again use a maths task to work out the probability of dying in an earthquake in various places around the world.

It is also possible to use this type of event as the basis for a drama lesson, considering perhaps how those who do not know where their loved ones are might react. How rescue attempts might be organized can be acted out and whether individuals might also try to rescue their friends and family without the help of aid agencies. Would this be a good or bad idea and what might happen without the right equipment? Possibly we might ask the class to consider how it might feel to be trapped underground. What thoughts might go through the mind? What might you hear? What would you do? This might be distressing but if undertaken carefully could be informative and an excellent teaching point.

Using biology and science

Teaching the life cycle without talking about the fact that all living things die is not teaching the whole subject. From the earliest experiences children see dead plants and dead animals and express a natural curiosity about them – so let's explain what is going on.

Starting with plant life we can discuss how the seed grows in a dark and warm atmosphere under the ground and sprouts out of the earth. It needs air, warmth and water to help it grow. It also needs nitrogen. As it grows it shows leaves and flowers. Eventually the flowers start to fade and the petals fall. The leaves also start to wither away and the plant begins to die. It may suffer from disease. It may suffer from the wrong condition such as too much sun or too much water. It may get attacked by predators. But it will eventually die.

Different plants live for different lengths of time. We might be aware of an ancient tree growing within the town. We can raise some quick-growing plants within the classroom and watch their progress and decay. What happens first to the plant when we notice it beginning to die? It may become discoloured. The leaves may lose moisture and become papery. It may wilt. Or we may not notice the progress because it happened rapidly.

We can then consider small animals and how they live and die. Depending on school policy it may be that the life cycle is taught from the point after birth – though if we use fish and worms it becomes less controversial for most schools working with young children.

- What do they need to help them live a healthy life?
- How is this like the plants?
- What are the differences?
- So what about when they get sick or old – what do we notice?
- Is this the same as with plants?
- How is it different?

We might ask who has seen a dead animal either on the roadside or in the garden. This allows those who want to talk about pets to do so, and those who prefer not to might talk about worms they have seen on the path or foxes on the roadside – which even in urban areas is not uncommon.

We can notice the texture of the skin or fur of the animal when it is dead, as we did with the plant. Here we can also notice that the animal will be cold – which we will not have noticed with the plants. What properties do animals have when they are living? If we are considering lower orders of animal we will consider what senses they might have. Can worms hear? They are aware of rain – but how do they become aware that it is raining? So we can discuss what senses animals might have. They can move, which plants cannot do. When they do not move they might be asleep or they might be dead. So what is the difference? There is a big difference between sleeping and being dead – so what are the differences? Normally with the higher order of animals they can hear, smell, see, feel things like hot and cold, and make sounds. When these senses are no longer present they are no longer sentient and therefore dead. We might consider animals that hibernate and how we tell the difference between the state of an animal in hibernation and a dead animal.

Using drama

History, health, PSHE, discussion material

Drama lessons offer endless opportunities to explore a wide range of issues surrounding death and loss. They can consider factual information as well as looking at the emotional aspects of loss and bereavement.

If one were looking at the ancient Egyptians it is easy to see how this could connect with current day practices on how we deal with the dead. Imagine that you are on an expedition in

Egypt with Howard Carter, exploring the pyramids. You already know some of things you hope to find. This is a special day when you are about to uncover the tomb of Tutenkhamun.

- What sort of thoughts go through your head?
- What do you say to each other?
- Do you know about the curse that is supposed to be on the tomb?

At this point we might consider why curses or bad things might be associated with the dead. Perhaps it is merely to keep people out, perhaps it is to do with protecting the dead, or perhaps it is fear of the dead.

- Do we have this type of superstition?
- Do we sometimes think that graveyards or tombs are frightening?

We then go into the chamber where the mummy of the king is concealed.

- What does it look like?
- How do we describe it?
- Is it like a coffin we might recognize today?
- How is it different?
- Would it be like this for the ordinary Egyptians?
- What will we see if we open it?
- Should we open it?
- What do we expect to find?
- What might stop us from opening it up?

Inside there is a body wrapped in cloth, but it is clearly the shape of a person.

- What if we looked in a coffin today – would the body be wrapped up in the same way?
- How would it be wrapped or clothed?

If we had the right equipment we could unwrap the body of Tutenkhamun.

- What would we find?
- How would it have been preserved?
- Is this what happens to bodies that are embalmed today?
- Does everybody get embalmed?
- Did they in ancient Egypt?

Through this piece of work it would be possible to make sense of how an ancient civilization treated its dead – or at least its rich dead – and consider how this makes sense to us by comparing it with modern practices. It might also make sense and demystify the modern practices of burial by placing them in a historical and cultural context.

Another way to consider how we think about death is by looking at funeral rites. We might think of recreating a funeral cortège from the Victorian era.

- What do we need?
- How will people be dressed?
- What colours will they be wearing?
- Will the coffin be carried by people or drawn by horses?
- Will the mourners be the family and friends of the deceased or will there be professional mourners?
- How will they behave?

- Will there be lots of crying and wailing or will there be no noise?

- Is this the same as nowadays?

- How is it different?

We might use a story in which one of the characters dies to stimulate thinking about how people react to loss and how they want to mark the loss of someone or something special. There are many children's stories in which characters die. In *Black Beauty* (Sewell 1954) there is a moving passage about the death of Merrylegs. Many children will have experienced the death of a pet and it could be useful to re-enact the scene to consider how the loss of a pet who is really a friend is an important event – but not one that is always acknowledged. There are many books written for children that look at death specifically and these might be used as the basis of the drama. Television and news articles might equally be the stimulus for drama. The purpose is to allow the children to ask questions and to consider what they think the answers are. Sometimes there will be no definite answers, but thoughts about attitudes and feelings. At other times it will be possible to give factual information.

Key points

- ◆ Normalizing talk of death in the classroom
- ◆ Using the National Curriculum to talk about death
- ◆ The Victorians
- ◆ Rites of passage and festivals
- ◆ Unexpected news
- ◆ Using number
- ◆ Using film and the media
- ◆ Using biology and science
- ◆ Using drama

References

Anthony, S. (1940) *The Child's Discovery of Death.* London: Kegan Paul, Trench, Trubner and Co.

Benefits Agency (1997) *D49 What to Do After a Death in England and Wales.* London: The Stationery Office.

Bowlby, J. (1963) 'Pathological mourning and childhood.' *Journal of the American Psychoanalytic Association 11*, 500–541.

Bowlby, J. (1969) *Attachment and Loss, Vol. 1 Attachment.* London: Hogarth Press.

Bowlby, J. (1981) *Attachment and Loss, Vol. 3 Loss.* London: Pimlico.

Clark, D. (1999) 'Death in Staithes.' In D. Dickenson and M. Johnson (eds) *Death, Dying and Bereavement.* London: Sage.

Dickenson, D. and Johnson, M. (eds) (1999) *Death, Dying and Bereavement.* London: Sage.

Durkheim, E. (1952) *Suicide: A Study in Sociology.* London: Routledge and Kegan Paul.

Feifel, H. (1959) *The Meaning of Death.* New York: McGraw-Hill.

Freud, S. (1917) *Mourning and Melancholia.* Collected Papers Standard Edition, vol.14. London: Institute of Psychoanalysis, 243–58.

Grainger, R. (1998) *The Social Symbolism of Grief and Mourning.* London: Jessica Kingsley Publishers.

GRO (Scotland) (1999) *Annual Report.* London: The Stationery Office.

Hertz, R. (1960) *Death and the Right Hand.* New York: Free Press.

Kubler-Ross, E. (1970) *On Death and Dying.* London: Tavistock.

Mead, M. (1928) *Coming of Age in Samoa: A Study of Adolescence and Sex in Primitive Societies.* Harmondsworth: Penguin.

Moore, O. (1996) PWA: *Looking Aids in the Face.* London: Picador.

Nagy, M. (1948) 'The child's theories concerning death.' In J. Bowlby (ed) (1980) *Loss: Sadness and Depression.* London: Penguin.

Nicholson, W. (1989) *Shadowlands.* London: Samuel French.

Piaget, J. (1954) *The Construction of Reality in the Child.* New York: Basic Books.

Robertson, J. (1953) *A Guide to the Film 'A Two Year Old Goes to Hospital'.* London: Tavistock.

Sewell, A (1954) *Black Beauty.* Harmondsworth: Puffin Books.

Thomas, D. (1952) 'Do not go gentle into that good night.' In *The Collected Poems.* New York: New Directions.

Winnicott, D. (1986) *Home is Where We Start From: Essays by a Psychoanalyst.* London: Penguin.

Worden, W. (1989) *Grief Counselling.* London: Routledge.

Further Reading

Albery, N., Elliot G. and Elliot, J. (eds) (1993) *The Natural Death Handbook.* London: Virgin Books.

Aries, P. (1974) *The Hour of Our Death.* London: Allen Lane.

Beit-Hallahmi, B. and Argle, M. (1997) *The Psychology of Religious Behaviour, Belief and Experience.* London: Routledge.

Bowker, J. (1991) *The Meanings of Death.* Cambridge: Cambridge University Press.

Collins, D., Tank, M. and Basith, A. (1993) *A Concise Guide to Customs of Minority Ethnic Religions.* Aldershot: Arena.

Feifel, H. (1977) *The New Meaning of Death.* New York: McGraw-Hill.

Fox, J. and Gill, S. (1997) *The Dead Good Funerals Guide.* Ulverston: Welfare State International.

Hockley, J.L. (1990) *Experiences of Death.* New York: Columbia University Press.

Isaacs, S. (1930) *Intellectual Growth in Young Children.* London: Routledge and Kegan Paul.

Nuland Sherwin, B. (1994) *How We Die.* London: Chatto and Windus.

Payne, S., Horn, S. and Relf, M. (1999) *Loss and Bereavement.* Buckingham: Open University Press.

Picardie, R. (1998) *Before I Say Goodbye.* London: Penguin.

Rollason, H. (1998) *Hope for Helen.* BBC 1, October. QED documentary.

Young, M. and Cullen, L. (1996) *A Good Death.* London: Routledge.

Books for children

Blume, J. (1987) *Tiger Eyes*. Scarsdale, NY: Bradbury Press.

Bunting, E. (1982) *The Happy Funeral*. New York: Harper and Row.

Graeber, C. (1982) *Mustard*. New York: Macmillan.

Gray, N. and Cabban, V. (2000) *Little Bear's Grandad*. London: Little Tiger Press.

Grindley, S. (1997) *Little Elephant Thunderfoot*. London: Orchard Books.

Hickman, M.W. (1984) *Last Week My Brother Anthony Died*. New York: Abingdon Press.

Schotter, R. (1979) *A Matter of Time*. New York: Collins Press.

Sewell, A. (1954) *Black Beauty*. Harmondsworth: Puffin Books.

Shook-Hazen, B. (1985) *Why Did Grandpa Die?* Racine, WI: Western Publishing.

Simmonds, P. (1988) *Fred*. London: Red Fox.

Smith, D.B. (1992) *A Taste of Blackberries*. Boston: Thomas Cromwell Press.

Varley, S. (1993) *Badger's Parting Gifts*. London: Hamilton.

Resources

Useful names and addesses

Natural Death Centre
20 Heber Road
London
NW2 6AA
www.naturaldeath.org.uk

Benefits Agency
Dept. of Social Security or TSO
The Causeway
Oldham Broadway Business Park
Chadderton
Oldham
OL9 9KD

University courses

Open University
School of Health and Social Welfare
Walton Hall
Milton Keynes
MK6 7AA
www.open.ac.uk

University of Reading
Whiteknights
PO Box 217
Reading
Berks
RG6 6AH
www.rdg.ac.uk

University of Wales: Lampeter
Dept. of Theology and Religious Studies
Lampeter
SA48 7CD
www.lampeter.ac.uk/trs

Websites

http://iul.com/raindrop

www.agitator.com

www.angelfire.com

www.bmj.com

www.britishcouncil.org/health

www.demographics.com

www.dundee.ac.uk/forensicmedicine

www.dying.abo

www.fortnet.org/Widownet

www.gidc.com/deathpen.htm

www.infoplease.com

www.leyhs.w-cook.k12.il.us/MIC/96-97/Group05/mum.htm

www.library.thinkquest.org

www.mwsc.edu/~hist

www.save.org

www.scotland.gov.uk/library/documents

www.teacher.deathpenaltyinfo.msu.edu

www.trinity.edu/~mkearl/death-2.html

www.uio.no/~mostarke/forens_ent/

www.unicef.org

Index

abdomen 30
abnormal grieving 99
absence of life 23–4
acceptance 41, 103
accidental death 50–1, 65, 104
accidents 52–3
action films 120
adolescence/adolescents 106
  concept of death (self-absorbed –
    formal operational stage) 96
adults' assumptions about children's grief
  90–1, 93
aerobic action of muscles 44
after death 43–9
ageing 24, 25, 29
AIDS 33, 34
  and dying 37–40
air crash, deaths from 17
air passages, blocked 30
alcohol 47, 60
Albert, Prince 16, 111
Allah 83
'all gone' (child's concept of death at
  sensory-motor stage) 95
All Saints Day 115
alms, giving 84
altruistic suicide 59
alveoli 39
ambulance staff 68
anaerobic action of muscles 44
anatomical research, use of bodies in 55,
  113
Anatomy Act 113
ancient Egyptians 48, 76, 123, 125
anger 32, 41, 91, 99, 101, 106
angina 27
animals 22–3, 46, 47, 94, 117, 121,
  122–3, 126
  see also pets
aninum 80
anniversary of death 84

anomic suicide 59
anoxia 29
answer same question several times, be
  prepared to 107
antarabhava 88
Anthony, S. 95
antibiotics 37
anti-viral treatments 39
anxiety 9, 53, 98, 104–8, 109
aromatherapy 64
art 114, 121
arteries
  blocked 30
  hardening of 26–7
ashes 102
  no scattering of 86, 88
  scattering of 82, 84
asking questions about death 9
asphyxia 29
asphyxiation 54, 121
assisted bathing 64
atheroma 26
atman 83
atrium 26
attachment
  and falling in love 98
  theory 90, 97–9
attention of adults, rejecting or craving
  106
autopsy 46, 65
avoiding 21

babytalk 106
bacteria 37–8, 45
Balkans 113
bargaining 41
Bart, Lionel 114
bathing 85
  ceremony 88
bedwetting 106
beetles 46
behaviours in grieving child, common
  106–8
beheading see decapitation
Beijing 112
benign tumours 36

Lightning Source UK Ltd.
Milton Keynes UK
30 October 2010

162122UK00002B/15/P